Total Quality Management (TQM)

Stress and Human Performance

Total Quality Management (TQM)

Stress and Human Performance

(including Case Studies)

Enugala Manohar

Faculty Member,
Department of Commerce and Business Management,
Satavahana University,
Karimnagar, Andhra Pradesh.

New Century Publications
New Delhi, India

NEW CENTURY PUBLICATIONS
4800/24, Bharat Ram Road,
Ansari Road, Daryaganj,
New Delhi – 110 002 (India)

Tel.: 011-2324 7798, 4358 7398, 6539 6605
Fax: 011-4101 7798
E-mail: indiatax@vsnl.com • info@newcenturypublications.com
www.newcenturypublications.com

Editorial office:
LG–7, Aakarshan Bhawan,
4754-57/23, Ansari Road, Daryaganj,
New Delhi – 110 002

Tel.: 011-4356 0919

First Published: **2012**

ISBN: **978-81-7708-302-6**

Published by New Century Publications and printed at Salasar Imaging Systems, New Delhi.

Designs: Patch Creative Unit, New Delhi.

PRINTED IN INDIA

In Loving Memory of My Mum

Shrimati E. Sarojana
and
Loving Son Randy Simon

I Dedicate this Book to My Dad
Rev. E. Anandam

About the Book

Organizational stress has become a crucial challenge for contemporary business undertakings. There is adequate empirical evidence which indicates a strong correlation between organizational stress and total quality management (TQM).

TQM programmes had their origins in the US companies in the 1980s in response to the competitive onslaught of Japanese companies in the automobile and electronics industries. Companies in many other industries quickly followed suit, as did the consulting firms to help companies adopt TQM. TQM is viewed as the continuous improvement of work processes to enhance an organization's ability to deliver high quality products/services in a cost-effective manner. It typically involves a number of interventions like identification of customer requirements, cross functional teams, selection of suppliers based on quality, and use of a variety of technical (scientific) methods to enhance analysis and process management methods. TQM also involves a multiple stakeholder philosophy which values community, customers and employees equally. Implicit in this philosophy are values of teamwork and collaboration.

There is little doubt that when implemented properly, TQM can have a dramatic impact on the performance and culture of an organization.

Author's Profile

Dr. Enugala Manohar is a faculty member, Department of Commerce and Business Management, Satavahana University, Karimnagar, Andhra Pradesh. He did his M.Phil. and Ph.D. from Kakatiya University. He has published a number of articles in leading journals. He has participated and presented papers at various national and international seminars/conferences including Advanced Leadership Seminar in Hawaii, USA from June 10 to July 5, 2007.

Contents

Preface

Work-related stress is a pattern of physiological, emotional, cognitive and behavioural reactions to some extremely taxing aspects of work content, work organization and work environment. When people experience work-related stress, they often feel tense and distressed and feel they cannot cope. Due to globalisation and changes in the nature of work, people in developing countries have to deal with increasing work-related stress. In industrialized countries people are becoming more familiar with what work-related stress is and how to manage it, however, in developing countries, this may not yet be the case. Although a few studies have been conducted in developing countries, particularly in Latin America, there are still not enough in-depth studies to fully analyse both cultural differences and behaviours which vary from one country to another. Along with existing difficulties in controlling other more well-known occupational risks, there is a lack of awareness of work-related stress, and shortage of resources to deal with it.

There is adequate empirical evidence which indicates a strong correlation between organizational stress and total quality management (TQM).

Total Quality Management (TQM) programmes had their origins in the U.S. companies in the 1980s in response to the competitive onslaught of Japanese companies in the automobile and electronics industries. Companies in many other industries quickly followed suit, as did the consulting firms to help companies adopt TQM. TQM is viewed as the continuous improvement of work processes to enhance an organization's ability to deliver high quality products/services in a cost-effective manner. It typically involves a number of interventions like identification of customer requirements, cross functional teams, selection of suppliers based on quality, use of a variety of technical (scientific) methods to enhance analysis and process management methods. TQM also involves a multiple stakeholder philosophy that values community, customers and employees equally. Implicit in this philosophy are values of teamwork and collaboration.

There is little doubt that when implemented properly, TQM can have a dramatic impact on the performance and culture of an organization.

Acknowledgements

I am deeply indebted to late Professor Ghanshyam Das Ojha who extended his co-operation with scholarly advise, meticulous care and warm personal affection. I also express my gratitude to Professor Mohd. Iqbal Ali and Professor G. Laxmaiah, Vice-chancellor and Registrar respectively of Satavahana University, Karimnagar for their enormous support and encouragement.

It is my good fortune to thank my parents, loving life partner and my family members for their encouragement and support to my academic pursuits.

I take the privilege to express my sincere gratitude to New Century Publications, New Delhi for agreeing to publish this book and extending all help and co-operation.

Karimnagar **Enugala Manohar**
October 2011

1

Management of Stress in Organisations

1.1 What is Stress?

Stress is a dynamic condition in which an individual is confronted with an opportunity, constraint or demand related to what he or she desires and for which the outcome is perceived to be both uncertain and important. While stress at work will remain a major challenge to occupational health, our ability to understand and manage that challenge is improving. Work stress is recognised world-wide as a major challenge to worker's health and the healthiness of their organisations. Workers who are stressed are also more likely to be unhealthy, poorly motivated, less productive and less safe at work. Their organisations are less likely to be successful in a competitive market.

Stress can be brought about by pressure at home and work. Employers cannot usually protect workers from stress arising outside of work, but they can protect them from stress that arises through work. Stress at work can be a real problem to the organisation as well as for its workers. Good management and good work organisations are the best forms of stress prevention. If the employees are already stressed, their managers should be aware of it and know how to help. This response can be observed through several different measures, including elevated heart rate, dilated pupils, increased blood pressure, and galvanic skin response (GSR) (which measures the electrical conductivity of the skin that changes when an individual is aroused or stressed). At least part of the physiological response to stressors is adaptive, a way for the body to prepare itself to function effectively under a challenging situation. For example, the increase in heart rate and rise in blood pressure are caused by the release of adrenaline and are intended to stimulate the central nervous system in preparation for performance. As a result, the stress response is often referred to as an adaptive one (Selye, 1993) [1].

Work-related stress is the response people may have when presented with work demands and pressures that are not matched to their knowledge and abilities which challenge their ability to cope. Stress occurs in a wide range of work circumstances but is often made worse when employees feel they have little support from supervisors and colleagues and where they have little control over work or how they can cope with its demands and pressures. Job stress in organizations is widespread. About half of all American workers feel the pressures of job-related stress. Extensive research shows that excessive job stress can adversely affect the emotional and physical health of workers. The result is decreased productivity, less satisfied, and less healthy workers.

1.2 Pressure and Stress

There is often confusion between pressure or challenge and stress and sometimes it is used to excuse bad management practices. Pressure at the work place is unavoidable due to the demands of the contemporary work environment. Pressure perceived as acceptable by an individual, may even keep workers alert, motivated, able to work and learn, depending on the available resources and personal characteristics. However, when that pressure becomes excessive or otherwise unmanageable it leads to stress. Stress can damage worker's health and business performance.

Stress results from a mismatch between the demands and pressures on the person, on the one hand, and their knowledge and abilities. This includes not only situations where the pressures of work exceed the worker's ability to cope but also where the worker's knowledge and abilities are not sufficiently utilised and that is a problem for them. A healthy job is likely to be one where the pressures on employees are appropriate in relation to their abilities and resources, to the amount of control they have over their work, and to the support they receive from people who matter to them. As health is not merely the absence of disease or infirmity but a positive state of complete physical, mental and social well-being (WHO, 1986) [2], a healthy working environment is one in which there is not only an absence of harmful conditions but an abundance of health promoting ones.

These may include continuous assessment of risks to health, the provision of appropriate information and training on health issues and the availability of health promoting organisational support practices and structures. A healthy work environment is one in which staff have made health and health promotion a priority and part of their working lives. The experience of stress is partly dependent on the individual's ability to cope with the demands placed on them by their work, and on the way in which they subsequently cope with those demands, and relates issues of control and support. More information is required on the nature, structure and effectiveness of individuals' abilities to meet work demands and to cope with any subsequent stress. The need for more information on coping is widely recognised (Dewe, 2000) [3], but relatively less attention has been paid to the need better to understand the concept of work ability or competence, although this is being flagged in relation to ageing research (Griffiths, 1999 [4] a; Ilmarinen and Rantanen, 1999 [5]).

1.3 Stress is an Imprecise Term

The definition of stress is not simply a question of semantics playing with words and it is important that there is agreement, at least in broad terms, on its nature. A lack of such agreement would seriously hamper research into stress and the subsequent development of effective stress management strategies. The term stress has many definitions, (Lazarus and Folkman, 1984) [6] defines stress as an internal state which can be caused by physical demands on the body or by environmental and social situations which are evaluated as potentially harmful, uncontrollable, or exceeding our resources for coping. The physical, environmental, and social causes of the stress state are termed stressors. Once induced by stressors, the internal stress state can lead to various responses. On the other hand, it can result in a number of physical, bodily responses, and also psychological responses such as anxiety, hopelessness, depression, irritability, and a general feeling of not being able to cope with the world can result from the stress state.

Stress is an imprecise term. It is usually defined in terms of the internal and external conditions that create stressful situations, and the symptoms that people experience when they are stressed. McGrath (1976) [7] proposed a definition based on the conditions necessary for stress. So there is a potential for stress when an environmental situation is perceived as presenting a demand that threatens to exceed the person's capabilities and resources for meeting it, under conditions where he expects a substantial differential in the rewards and costs from meeting the demand versus not meeting it. McGrath's definition implies that the degree of stress is correlated with a person's perceived inability to deal with an environmental demand. This would lead to the conclusion that a person's level of stress depends on their self-perceived abilities and self-confidence. Stress is correlated with a person's fear of failure. Arnold and Feldman (1986) [8] define stress as “the reactions of individuals to new or threatening factors in their work environment” (p. 459) since our work environments often contain new situations, this definition suggests that stress is inevitable. This definition also highlights the fact that reactions to stressful situations are individualized, and can result in emotional, perceptual, behavioural, and physiological changes.

Williams and Huber (1986) [9] define stress as “a psychological and physical reaction to prolonged internal and environmental conditions in which an individual's adaptive capabilities are overextended" (p. 243). They argue that stress is an adaptive response to a conscious or unconscious threat. Like McGrath, they point out that stress is a result of a "perceived" threat, and is not necessarily related to actual environmental conditions. The amount of stress that is produced by a given situation depends upon one's perception of the situation, not the situation itself. In other words, stress is a relativistic phenomenon. In Gestalt Therapy Verbatim (Real People Press, 1969) [10] Perls proposes a more general definition, where stress is a manifestation of thinking about the future.

1.4 Anxiety

Anxiety is created by focusing attention away from the "here and now". It is created by expectations of the future the tension between the now and the later. According to Perls, there is no difference between good stress and bad stress. They are both created by thinking about the future. When anxiety finds an outlet, we say that the stress was motivating; when it doesn't, we call it debilitating. French, Kast, and Rosenzweig (1985) [11] also emphasized the idea that stress itself is not necessarily bad. "The term stress can be considered neutral with the words distress and eustress used for designating bad and good effects" (p. 707). They propose a model that defines an optimum range of stress in terms of its effect on performance. Stress levels that exceed an optimum level result in decreased performance and eventual burnout. Stress levels below a minimum level result in decreased performance and "rust-out".

Stress in individual is defined as any interference that disturbs a persons' healthy mental and physical well being. It occurs when the body is required to perform beyond its normal range of capabilities. Stress is the way that a person react physically, mentally and emotionally to various conditions, changes and demands in his life. High levels of stress can affect his physical and mental well being and performance. Stress is a dynamic condition, which an individual is confronted with an opportunity, constraint or demand related to what he or she desires and for which the outcome is perceived to be both uncertain and important. Stress is associated with constraints and demands. The former prevents from doing what a person desires, the latter refers to the loss of something desired. Stress is highest for those individuals who perceive that they are uncertain as to whether they will win or lose and lowest for those individuals who think that winning or losing is certainty.

Canadian physician Hans Selye (1907-1982) in his book the stress of life 1956 popularized the idea of stress. Selye (1956) [12] defines stress as a non-specific response of the body to any sort of demand made on it. Selye defines this "demand," which could include a stimulus or an event, as a stressor and notes that a wide variety of stimuli are capable of producing the same internal stress response. Stressors are external and can come in several different forms, ranging from extreme temperature to a physical assault. According to Selye, once the individual has been exposed to the stressor, a physiological stress response will occur.

The simple equating of demand with stress has been associated with the belief that a certain amount of stress is linked to maximum performance and possibly good health. Belief in optimal levels of stress has been used, on occasions, to justify poor management practices. Given this, it is an unfortunate but popular misconception that there is little consensus on the definition of stress as a scientific concept or, worse, that stress is in some way indefinable and immeasurable. This belief belies a lack of knowledge of the relevant scientific literature. The results of stress are harmful to individuals, families, society and organizations, which can suffer from "organization stress". However, Mandler (1993) [13] argues that a definition focusing on the physiological aspects of stress is too narrow. He suggests that "stress" refers most appropriately to the convergence of the physiological and psychological effects of stressors. He maintains that only when stressors and their physiological responses affect behaviour, thought, or action do they become relevant to the stress concept. In order to have true notion on stress, there are various approaches which can reveal the nature of stress. They are as follows.

The first approach conceptualises occupational stress as an aversive or noxious characteristic of the work environment, and, in related studies, treats it as an independent variable the environmental cause of ill health. This has been termed the 'engineering approach'.

The second approach, on the other hand, defines stress in terms of the common physiological effects of a wide range of aversive or noxious stimuli. It treats stress as a dependent variable as a particular physiological response to a threatening or damaging environment. This has been termed the 'physiological approach'.

The third approach conceptualises work stress in terms of the dynamic interaction between the person and their work environment. When studied, stress is either inferred from the existence of problematic person-environment interactions or measured in terms of the cognitive processes and emotional reactions which underpin those interactions. This final approach has been termed the 'psychological approach'. The engineering and physiological approaches are obvious among the earlier theories of stress, while the more psychological approaches characterise contemporary stress theory.

1.5 Engineering Approach to Stress

The engineering approach has treated stress as a stimulus characteristic of the person's environment, usually conceived in terms of the load or level of demand placed on the individual, or some aversive (threatening) or noxious element of that environment (Cox, 1978 [14], 1990 [15]; Fletcher, 1988 [16]). Occupational stress is treated as a property of the work environment, and usually as an objectively measurable aspect of that environment. In 1947, Symonds wrote, in relation to psychological disorders in the Royal Air Force flying personnel, that "stress is that which happens to the man, not that which happens in him; it is a set of causes not a set of symptoms."

Somewhat later, Spielberger (1976) [17] argued, in the same vein, that the term stress should refer to the objective characteristics of situations. According to this approach, stress was said to produce a strain reaction which although often reversible could, on occasions, prove to be irreversible and damaging (Sutherland and Cooper, 1990) [18]. The concept of a stress threshold grew out of this way of thinking and individual differences in this threshold have been used to account for differences in stress resistance and vulnerability.

1.6 Physiological Approach to Stress

The physiological approach to the definition and study of stress received its initial impetus from the work of Selye (1950 [19], 1956 [20]). He defined stress as "a state manifested by a specific syndrome which consists of all the non-specific changes within the biologic system" that occur when challenged by aversive or noxious stimuli. Stress is treated as a generalised and non specific physiological response syndrome. For many years, the stress response was largely conceived of in terms of the activation of two neuro-endocrine systems, the anterior pituitary-adrenal cortical system and the sympathetic-adrenal medullary system (Cox and Cox, 1985) [21]. Selye (1950) [22] argued that the physiological response was triphasic in nature involving an initial alarm stage (sympathetic adrenal medullary activation) followed by a stage of resistance (adrenal cortical activation) giving way, under some circumstances, to a final stage of exhaustion (terminal reactivation of the sympathetic adrenal medullary system).

Repeated, intense or prolonged elicitation of this physiological response, it has been suggested, increases the wear and tear on the body, and contributes to what Selye (1956) [23] has called the 'diseases of adaptation'. This apparently paradoxical term arises from the contrast between the immediate and short-term advantages bestowed by physiological response to stress (energy mobilisation for an active behavioural response) to the long-term disadvantages (increased risk of certain 'stress related' diseases). Scheuch (1996) [24] considers stress as one of the psycho-physiological activities of human beings as they attempt to adapt to changes in the internal and external milieu. This activity relates to the quantity and quality of the relationship between demands and individual somatic, psychological and social capacities or resources in a specific material and social environment. Stress is understood by Scheuch as a reactive activity to a disturbed homeostatic state of organic functions, psychological functions and/or in the interaction between the human being and his or her social environment. The adaptation follows the principles of economisation of function, the principle of minimisation of effort, and the principle of well-being. Stress itself is the expression of a disorder of these principles (Scheuch, 1990 [25], 1996) [26].

1.7 Psychological Approach

The third approach to the definition and study of stress conceptualises it in terms of the dynamic interaction between the person and their work environment. When studied, it is either inferred from the existence of problematic person-environment interactions or measured in terms of the cognitive processes and emotional reactions which underpin those interactions. This has been termed the 'psychological approach'. The development of psychological models has been, to some extent, an attempt to overcome the criticisms levelled at the earlier approaches. There is now a consensus developing around this approach to the definition of stress. For example, psychological approaches to the definition of stress are largely consistent with the International Labour Office's definition of psychosocial hazards (International Labour Organization, 1986) [27] and with the definition of well-being recommended by the World Health Organization (1986) [28].

They are also consistent with the developing literature on personal risk assessment (see, for example, Cox and Cox, 1993 [29]; Cox & Griffiths, 1995) [30]. These consistencies and overlaps suggest an increasing coherence in current thinking within occupational health and safety. Variants of this psychological approach dominate contemporary stress theory, and among them two distinct types can be identified: the interactional and the transactional. The former focus on the structural features of the person's interaction with their work environment, while the latter are more concerned with the psychological mechanisms underpinning that interaction. Transactional models are primarily concerned with cognitive appraisal and coping. In a sense they represent a development of the interactional models, and are essentially consistent with them.

Job stress can be defined as the harmful physical and emotional responses that occur when the requirements of the job do not match the capabilities, resources, or needs of the worker. Job stress can lead to poor health and even injury. The concept of job stress is often confused with challenge, but these concepts are not the same. Challenge energizes us psychologically and physically, and it motivates us to learn new skills and master our jobs. When a challenge is met, we feel relaxed and satisfied. Thus, challenge is an important ingredient for healthy and productive work. The importance of challenge in our work lives is probably what people are referring to when they say a little bit of stress is good for you.

Nearly everyone agrees that job stress results from the interaction of the worker and the conditions of work. Views differ, however, on the importance of worker characteristics versus working conditions as the primary cause of job stress. These differing viewpoints are important because they suggest different ways to prevent stress at work. Performance directly contributes to work satisfaction and is a direct result of effort, and not vice versa. In order to increase work motivation, stress should be laid on increasing employees' effort for good performance.

As NIOSH (National Institute for Occupational Safety and Health) job stress can be defined as the harmful physical and emotional responses that occur when the requirements of the job do not match the capabilities, resources, or needs of the worker. Job stress can lead to poor health and even injury. The demands of today's employment environment play a major role in the stress that affects workers. Technology that is evolving at breakneck speed, mergers, takeovers and layoffs, increased productivity requirements and internal reorganizations are part of the daily life of managers and employees alike. The tension caused by these changes can challenge the psychological balance of workers and have a negative impact on their health, especially when the changes involve work overload, lack of participation in decision-making process or even a lack of recognition of the individual or the work done.

On the basis of experience and research NIOSH favours the view that working conditions play a primary role in causing job stress. However, the role of individual factors is not ignored. According to NIOSH view, exposure to stressful working conditions (called job stressors) can have a direct influence on worker safety and health. Individual and other situational factors can intervene to strengthen or weaken this influence. There is a need to care for ill employees which is a situational factor that may intensify the effects of stressful working conditions. Individual and situational factors that can help to reduce the effects of stressful working conditions include the following:

- Balance between work and family or personal life;
- A support network of friends and co-workers; and
- A relaxed and positive outlook.

According to one school of thought, differences in

individual characteristics such as personality and coping style are most important in predicting whether certain job conditions will result in stress-in other words, what is stressful for one person may not be a problem for someone else. This viewpoint leads to prevention strategies that focus on workers and ways to help them cope with demanding job conditions.

Stress can be defined as a psychological state which is part of and reflects a wider process of interaction between the person and their work environment. It is concluded that there is a growing consensus around the adequacy and utility of the psychological approach to stress. Several overview models have been offered as summaries of the stress process. The most notable is that of Cooper (see, for example, Cooper and Marshall, 1976). Cooper's model usefully focuses on the nature and detail of work stresses and their individual and organisational outcomes. The stress state is a conscious state but the level of awareness of the problem varies with the development of that state. Part of the stress process are the relationships between the objective work environment and the employee's perceptions of work, between those perceptions and the experience of stress, and between that experience and changes in behaviour and physiological function, and in health. Coping is an important component of the stress process but one which is relatively poorly understood. Stress may be experienced as a result of exposure to a wide range of work demands and, in turn, contribute to an equally wide range of health outcomes: it is one link between hazards and health.

In 2001, the HSE (Health and Safety Executive) published a guide for managers running units or departments with 50 or more staff. The guide focused on the application of a structured approach to stress prevention by providing a five-step work-related stress risk assessment to aid diagnosis of the problems and provide a framework for intervention. This model is developed based on earlier 'engineering' models of stress, which includes the main stress-related hazards and outcomes.

1.8 Role of Anxiety in Stress

Anxiety is the negative emotional state with feelings of worry, nervousness, and apprehension associated with activation of the body.

The amount of excitement, or the degree to which one is "stirred up"; indicated by the electroencephalogram, galvanic skin response, muscle tension etc.; influenced by activity in the ascending reticular activating system and the sympathetic system. Many emotions have an arousal component. When we are emotional, we often feel excited.

Moment to moment changes in worries and negative thoughts in cognitive state anxiety and moment to moment changes in perceived physiological arousal. Anxiety and arousal are the indicators of the stress. Anxiety is the root cause for development of stress. With anxiety a person can perceive wide range of objectively non dangerous circumstances as threatening and to respond to these with disproportionate state anxiety levels. Arousal is a general physiological and psychological activation of the organism that varies on a continuum from seep sleep to intense excitement.

Most of life events fit into "guilt, fear and anger", the many life events starting with "change". A few questions also had grief involved, which might be the biggest stress factor. Even with the death of a spouse, there will often be associated feelings of guilt, anger and fear.

The Energy Draining Triad is addressed by these three questions, each dealing with one aspect of the Triad, to help the client experience a fresh breath of life leading to freedom from the energy draining feeling involved. Stress consists with these three factors like guilt, fear and anger.

1. What steps can I take to manage my guilt?
2. What steps can I take to manage my anger?
3. What steps can I take to manage my fear?

All these three questions are action oriented, "What steps can I take...". They talk about options, not burdens; not something I have to do, but something that I am choosing to do. This deals first and foremost thoughts and emotions, some times those thoughts are to be stopped, some times they need them captive and some times the action is to be taken.

1.9 Role of Stress and Stressor

Stress is the non-specific response of the body to any demands. Stress can be defined as our response (stress reactivity) to a stimulus (stressor). Stress is usually put into two different categories:

- Distress (from Latin dis = bad).
- Eustress (from Greek eu = good).

It is good stress when we are close to falling off the roof and our body goes in to a state of stress, which makes us more alert and helps us to act quickly. It is bad stress, when our minds cannot quiet down after a meeting, so that the adrenaline keeps rushing through our body. We cannot fall asleep, find rest and be refreshed. Body-Brain Boosters: Help in Managing Distress. People who manage their stress seem to have the following attitudinal qualities.

- They feel involved and committed (to life, work, and relationships).
- They feel open to change.
- They feel in control (of life, work, and relationships).

Of course, it's not easy to adopt a new attitude, but it is important to note that your attitude affects your stress levels. There are three factors which can help in managing distress

Commitment: Allow yourself to commit to the challenge, yourself and the people who are associated with the situation

Challenge: Try to look at a situation as a challenge rather than a threat. Talk to yourself (internally or out aloud), thinking about how a particular situation is threatening to you and possible reasons why. You may even learn a few things about yourself.

Control: Take control of events and the way people treat you by being assertive and communicating well. People cannot respond to you unless they know what is going on. In this context a positive attitude is a bonus. Turn negative thoughts into positive ones, try to stop seeing everything as dark and gloomy.

Stressor: A stressor is defined by Selye as "that which produces stress". This stressor can be external or internal. The external stressor could be an illness. An internal stressor could be worry about facing the next problem or perceived problematic situations. People experience stressors differently. It has to do with our perception of the situation and our body's response is proportional to the magnitude of the perceived danger or threat.

1.10 Characteristics of Stressor

Each event or situation has certain characteristics that determine the severity that the stressor may or may not have on us. A scale was developed to measure life stress and is measured in "life change units" (LCU). The characteristics of the stressor that influence how high it will be on the scale and the severity of stress which result include the following.

Significance: How critical and important the event is to the individual and how change will have to be dealt with. The greater the significance and change, the higher the impact of the stressor.

Time length: If a stressor is continued over a long period of time, it will result in higher stress levels.

Cumulative Effect: This is when stressors are built up over a period of time without appropriate mechanisms to reduce or release the build up.

Multiplicity: A number of stressors at one time will result in higher stress levels.

Approaching Deadline: If a demand has been made a few weeks or months in advance of the deadline, the degree of stress will increase as the due date approaches.

The general adaptation syndrome, response to stressors is divided into three stages: the alarm reaction, resistance, and exhaustion. The above black curve type line represents resistance to a continuous original stressor; the bottom curve type line represents resistance to a new stressor imposed in different stages of the adaptation syndrome.

Hans Selye (1956) [31] termed the body's response to stressors the general adaptation syndrome.

Alarm Reaction: The alarm reaction is essentially the emergency response of the body. In this stage, responses of the body, many of them mediated by the sympathetic nervous system, prepare us to cope with the stressor.

State of Resistance: If the stressor continuous to be present, the stage of resistance begins, wherein the body resists the effects of the continuous stressor.

Stage of Exhaustion: The final stage of the general adaptation syndrome is the stage of exhaustion. In this stage the body's capacity to respond to both continuous and new stressors has been seriously compromised. In this situation a person may no longer be able to ward off infection and may become sick and perhaps die. Or, because of other stressor-induced hormonal effects, stomach ulcers, diabetes, skin disorders, asthma, high blood pressure, increased susceptibility to cancer (Bammer and Newberry, 1983) [32] or a host of other diseases may occur at this stage or late in the stage of resistance (Selye, 1976 [33], Allen, 1983) [34].

Almost any change in the environment even a pleasant change, such as a vacation demands some coping; and a little stress is useful in helping us to adapt. But beyond some point "stress" becomes "distress". What acts to produce distress varies greatly from person to person, but some events seem to be stressors for many of us. Chief among these are injuries or infections of the body; annoying or dangerous events in our environments; major changes or transitions, in life which force us to cope in new ways, and anticipated or actual threats to our self-esteem.

Stress Cycle: Stress has a number of immediate effects and if the stressors are maintained, long-term behavioural, physiological, emotional, and cognitive (thinking) effects occur. If these effects hinder adaptation to the environment or create discomfort and distress, they themselves become stressors. On the other hand, many people have developed ways of coping with stressors so that they are able to respond adaptively.

1.11 Causes of Stress

Stressors can be divided into those that arise from within an individual (internal), and those that are attributable to the environment (external). Internal conflicts, non-specific fears, fears of inadequacy, and guilt feelings are examples of stressors that do not depend on the environment. Internal sources of stress can arise from an individual's perceptions of an environmental threat, even if no such danger actually exists. Environmental stressors are external conditions beyond an individual's control. Bhagat (1983) [35] has reported that work performance can be seriously impaired by external stressors. There are many aspects of organizational life that can become external stressors. These include issues of structure, management's use of authority, monotony, a lack of opportunity for advancement, excessive responsibilities, ambiguous demands, value conflicts, and unrealistic work loads. A person's non-working life (e.g., family, friends, health, and financial situations) can also contain stressors that negatively impact job performance.

Albrecht (1979) [36] argues that nearly all stressors are emotionally induced. These are based on peoples' expectations, or "the belief that something terrible is about to happen." (p. 83) Thus, emotionally induced stress arises from one's imagination. Albrecht believes that our society's number one health problem is anxiety, and that emotionally induced stress can be classified into four categories: (1) time stress, (2) anticipatory stress, (3) situational stress, and (4) encounter stress. Time stress is always created by a real or imaginary deadline. Anticipatory stress is created when a person perceives that an upcoming event will be unpleasant. Situational stress can occur when a person is in an unpleasant situation, and they worry about what will happen next. Encounter stress is created by contact with other people (both pleasant and unpleasant).

Many situations in organizational life can be stressful. These include: (1) problems with the physical environment, such as poor lighting or excessive nose, (2) problems with the quality of work such, as lack of diversity, an excessive pace, or too little work, (3) role ambiguities or conflicts in responsibilities, (4) relationships with supervisors, peers, and subordinates, and (5) career development stressors, such as lack of job security, perceived obsolescence, and inadequate advancement. French, Kast, and Rosenzweig (1985) [37] believe that any situation that requires a behavioural adjustment is a source of stress. However, a situation that is stressful for one person might not be stressful for another. Older workers seem to be less strongly affected by stressful situations. (Parasuraman and Alutto, 1984) [38] Individuals with high self-esteem and a tolerance for ambiguity are less prone to stress-related illnesses. There is also considerable evidence that a person's susceptibility to stress is dependent on their personality types. Type A personalities (those that seek out fast-paced, challenging situations) often react to stress with hostility and anger, while Type B personalities seem to be have an immunity to the same stressors (Albrecht, 1979 [39]; Friedman and Rosenman, 1974 [40]; Matthews, 1982 [41]; Organ, 1979) [42]. Meyer Friedman and Ray H. Rosenman researched the link between personality type, stress and heart disease.

Friedman and Rosenman (1974) [43] tested 2,500 people and 50-60 percent could be identified as authentic type A's. They also found that Type B personalities didn't have any heart problems before the age of 70. This personality profile has been re-tested (Goodheart, 1994) [44] and now the only characteristic held up as a predict of heart disease is unresolved hostility which is found as an encouraging factor.

1.12 Job Conditions Leading to Stress

Design of Tasks: Heavy workload, infrequent rest breaks, long work hours and shift work; hectic and routine tasks that have little inherent meaning, do not utilize workers' skills, and provide little sense of control.

Management Style: Lack of participation by workers in decision-making, poor communication in the organization, lack of family-friendly policies.

Interpersonal Relationships: Poor social environment and lack of support or help from co-workers and supervisors.

Work Roles: Conflicting or uncertain job expectations, too much responsibility, and too many "hats to wear."

Career Concerns: Job insecurity and lack of opportunity for growth, advancement, or promotion; rapid changes for which workers are unprepared.

Environmental Conditions: Unpleasant or dangerous physical conditions such as crowding, noise, air pollution, or ergonomic problems.

Although much of the research on the relationship between stress and functioning focuses on the negative performance effects of stress, not all stress is bad. In fact, Selye (1956) [45] emphasizes that stress is a necessary part of life and that it does not always involve negative consequences for the organism involved. In fact, at certain moderate levels, stress can actually improve individual performance. There is substantial research supporting the concept of "good stress." Yerkes and Dodson (1908) [46] were the first to "stumble" upon the inverted-U relationship between stress and performance. Their work focused on the effects of stress on the learning response of rats.

Using three trials with low, moderate, and high levels of stimulus, the authors find a weak but curvilinear relationship, with performance on the task improving as the stressor stimulus reached a moderate level and decreasing as stimulus strength increased beyond this point.

1.13 Potential Sources of Stress

There are three categories of potential stressors:

- Environmental factor,
- Organizational factor, and
- Individual factors.

Just as environmental uncertainty influences the design of an organization's structure, it also influences stress level among employees in that organization. Changes in the business cycle create economic uncertainties. When the economy is contracting, people become anxious about their security. Political uncertainties don't tend to create stress among employees directly but they do influence organizations. This would lead to creation of stress among employees in the organization. Technological factors are also going to influence organization which involves stress also. Organizational factors would cause stress to the employees. Pressures to avoid errors or complete tasks in a limited time period, work overload, a demanding and intensive boss, and unpleasant co-workers are a few examples. Then there are factors like task demands, role demands, interpersonal demands and organizational leadership. Every organization goes through a cycle. They are established; they grow, become mature, and eventually decline. An organization's life stage – that is, where it is in this four stage cycle creates different problems and pressures for employees. The establishment and decline stages are particularly stressful. The former is characterized by a great deal of excitement and uncertainty, while the later typically requires cutbacks, layoffs, and a different set of uncertainties. Stress tends to be least in maturity where uncertainties are at their lower ebb.

The typical individual only works about forty hours a week. The experiences and problems that people encounter in those other 128 non-work hours each week can spill over to the job. Our final category, then, encompasses factors that comprise the employee's personal life. Primarily, this focuses on family and personal economic problems. An economic problem created by individuals overextending their financial resources is another set of personal troubles that can create stress for employees and distract their attention from their work. Stress shows itself in a number of ways.

For instance, an individual who is experiencing a high level of stress may develop high blood pressures, ulcers, irritability, difficulty in making routine decisions, loss of appetite, accident proneness and the like. These can be subsumed under three general categories, physiological, psychological, and the behavioural symptoms.

1.14 Symptoms of Stress

Selye (1936) [47] was the first to describe the phases that the body goes through in response to a threat. The general adaptation syndrome model states that the body passes through three stages. The first stage is an alarm reaction. The body prepares for a potential emergency. Digestion slows down, the heart beats faster, blood vessels dilate, blood pressure rises, and breathing becomes rapid and deep. All bodily systems work together to provide maximum energy for fight or flight. The second stage is resistance. If the stress continues, the body builds up a tolerance to its effects. The body becomes habituated to the effects of the stressor, however, the bodies adaptive energies are being used as a shield against the stressor. The third stage is exhaustion. When the body's adaptive energies are depleted, the symptoms of the alarm reaction reappear, and the stress manifests itself as an illness, such as ulcers, heart ailments, and high blood pressure. During the first or second stages, the removal of the stressor will eliminate the symptoms.

Physiological Symptoms: Most of the early concern with stress was directed at physiological symptoms. This was predominantly due to the fact that the topic was researched by specialists in the health and medical sciences. This research led to the conclusion that stress could create changes in metabolism, increase heart and breathing rates, increase blood pressure, bring on headaches, and induce heart attacks.

Psychological Symptoms: Stress can cause dissatisfaction. Job-related stress can cause job-related dissatisfaction. Job dissatisfaction, in fact, is 'the simplest and most obvious psychological effect' from stress. But stress shows itself in other psychological states for instance, tension, anxiety, irritability, boredom, and procrastination.

Behavioural Symptoms: Behaviourally related stress symptoms include changes in productivity, absence, and turnover, as well as changes in eating habits, increased smoking or consumption of alcohol, rapid speech, fidgeting, and sleep disorders.

The American Institute of Stress, Information Sheet states there are 50 common sings and symptoms of stress.

1. Frequent headaches, jaw clenching or pain,
2. Gritting, grinding teeth,
3. Tremors, trembling of lips, hands,
4. Neck ache, back pain, muscle spasms,
5. Stuttering or stammering,
6. Light-headedness, faintness, dizziness,
7. Ringing, buzzing or "popping sounds",
8. Frequent blushing, sweating,
9. Cold or sweaty hands, feet,
10. Dry mouth, problems swallowing,
11. Frequent colds, infections, herpes sores,
12. Rashes, itching, hives, "goose bumps",
13. Unexplained or frequent "allergy" attacks,
14. Heartburn, stomach pain, nausea,
15. Excess belching, flatulence,
16. Constipation, diarrhoea, loss of control,
17. Difficulty breathing, frequent sighing,
18. Sudden attacks of life threatening panic,
19. Chest pain, palpitations, rapid pulse,
20. Frequent urination,

21. Diminished sexual desire or performance,
22. Excess anxiety, worry, guilt, nervousness,
23. Increased anger, frustration, hostility,
24. Depression, frequent or wild mood swings,
25. Increased or decreased appetite,
26. Insomnia, nightmares, disturbing dreams,
27. Difficulty concentration, racing thoughts,
28. Trouble learning new information,
29. Forgetfulness, disorganization, confusion,
30. Difficulty in making decisions,
31. Feeling overloaded or overwhelmed,
32. Frequent crying spells of suicidal thoughts,
33. Feeling of loneliness or worthlessness,
34. Little interest in appearance, punctuality,
35. Nervous habits, fidgeting, feet tapping,
36. Increased frustration, irritability, edginess,
37. Overreaction to petty annoyances,
38. Increased number of minor accidents,
39. Obsessive or compulsive behaviour,
40. Reduced work efficiency or productivity,
41. Lies or excuse to cover up poor work,
42. Rapid or mumbled speech,
43. Excessive defensiveness or suspiciousness,
44. Problems in communication, sharing,
45. Social withdrawal and isolation,
46. Constant tiredness, weakness, fatigue,
47. Frequent use of over-the-counter drugs,
48. Increased smoking, alcohol or drug use,
49. Weight gain or loss without diet, and
50. Excessive gambling or impulse buying.

1.15 Long-term Effects of Stress

When exposed to long term stress, the body will start to be affected.

1. Normally the thymus gland relaxes and expands. In the expansive state it functions to its peak; producing lymphocytes that contain cancer killing T-cells. The

thymus gland shrinks during long illness or periods of stress. Under prolonged stress we tend towards illness.

2. Dr. Hart (1999) [48] writes, "The anti-pain system becomes depleted. When the demand is unrelenting, the endorphins become depleted. This is one of the reasons why stress-related illness is so often linked to feelings of pain all over the body".
3. "The anti-anxiety systems become depleted. Under prolonged conditions of stress. However, these natural tranquillisers become depleted and the experience of anxiety goes up. This can make us prone to panic attack." (Dr. Hart, Archibald, 1991) [49].

The stress effects can take place in the following ways.

1. **Brain:** When a person feels stress the reaction in the body would take place like increased blood flow which awakes alert a person. This is the immediate reaction in the body.
2. **Heart:** The impact of stress will be on heart. Due to stress the reaction is the pulse rate or heart rate and increases and elevated blood pressure.
3. **Stomach:** The stress reaction on the body is the secretion of extra acid and accelerated digestions. With this a person gets acidity problem and chest burning would take place.
4. **Muscles:** Due to stress, there is extra blood supply, and increased tension. Stress consists of fear, guilt and anxiety. With this a person's body reaction is extra blood supply to muscles and increased tension.
5. **Lungs:** The stress reaction on the body is that increased level of oxygen in blood and removal of waste gas. Every movement whenever a person feels stress the stomach condition becomes upset and a person may not feel comfortable.
6. **Skin:** The stress impact on body is that sweat increases, blood is withdrawn from extremities and hands become cold. Due to more sweat a person feels thirsty all the times.

1.16 Effects of Work Stress on Organizations

If key staff or a large number of workers are affected,

work stress may challenge the healthiness and performance of their organisation. Unhealthy organisations do not get the best from their workers and this may affect not only their performance in the increasingly competitive market but eventually even their survival.

Work stress affects the organisations in the following ways:

1. Increased absenteeism,
2. Decreasing commitment to work,
3. Increasing staff turn-over,
4. Impairing performance and productivity,
5. Increasing unsafe working practices and accident rates,
6. Increasing complaints from clients and customers,
7. Adversely affecting staff recruitment,
8. Increasing liability to legal claims and actions by stressed workers, and
9. Damaging the organisation's image both among its workers and externally.

1.17 Workability and Coping

Coping is an important part of the overall stress process. However, it is perhaps the least well understood despite many years of research. This point is widely acknowledged in the literature (Dewe, 1993 [50], 2000) [51] Lazarus (1966) [52] has suggested that it has three main features.

First, it is a process: it is what the person actually thinks and does in a stressful encounter. Second, it is context-dependent: coping is influenced by the particular encounter or appraisal that initiates it and by the resources available to manage that encounter. Finally, coping as a process is and should be defined 'independent of outcome'; that is, independently of whether it was successful or not (Folkman, 1984 [53]; Lazarus and Folkman, 1984) [54]. There have been two approaches to the study of coping: that which attempts to classify the different types of coping strategies and produce a comprehensive taxonomy, and that which considers coping as a problem solving process (Dewe, 2000) [55].

We respond to whatever is stressful and threatening in two ways. The initial reaction is emotion-focused (level 1), meaning that we seek ways to cope with our feeling of distress. If it is possible to remove or modify the threat, however, a problem focused (level 2) type of coping can be employed.

1.18 Coping Taxonomies

Lazarus (1966) [56] has argued that the person usually employs both task and emotion focused coping strategies. The former attempt some form of action directly targeted at dealing with the source of stress (adaptation of the environment), while the latter attempt to attenuate the emotional experience associated with that stress (adaptation to the environment).

The perceived success, or otherwise, of such strategies feeds back into the appraisal process to alter the person's perception of the situation. Lazarus and his colleagues (Lazarus, 1966 [57]; Lazarus and Folkman, 1984) [58] also emphasise that the importance of the situation to the individual is critical in determining the intensity of their response. Dewe (1987) [59], in a typical study, examined sources of stress and strategies used to cope with them in ministers of religion in New Zealand. Using factor analytical techniques, he identified five clusters of coping strategies: seeking social support, postponing action by relaxation and distracting attention, developing greater ability to deal with the problem, rationalising the problem, and drawing on support through spiritual commitment.

It was possible to classify 33 percent of the strategies which made up these clusters as task focused and 67 percent as emotion focused. The most frequent source of stress experienced by the ministers related to the emotional and time difficulties associated with crisis work, and the experience of such problems appeared to be associated with coping by seeking social support and rationalising the problem.

Pearlin and Associates (Pearlin and Schooler, 1978 [60];

Pearlin et al., 1981) [61] have further developed this general approach and distinguished between responses concerned with changing the situation, those concerned with changing its meaning (re-appraisal) and those relating to the management of the symptoms of stress. In a different vein, Miller (1979) [62] has distinguished between two informational styles which she terms 'blunters' and 'monitors': the former tend to use denial strategies and the latter information seeking strategies in relation to stressful situations.

These and the many other classifications available in the literature are, generally, neither inconsistent nor meant to be mutually exclusive. Most authors emphasise that no one type of coping strategy is necessarily better than any other in solving a problem. People use a mixture of strategies in most situations, although certain situations may tend to be associated with particular types of strategy.

Some studies have tried to explore the existence of systematic links between stressors and coping styles, but found little empirical support for their hypotheses. Salo (1995) [63] found differences in teachers' ways of coping, but those differences related to the amount, not the source, of stress experienced, and the timing (changed throughout the autumn term).

Wykes and Whittington (1991) [64] studied the different ways in which psychiatric nursing staff dealt with incidents of violent physical assault. They found that each respondent reported an average three distinct coping strategies. These studies seem to support the existence of complex, dynamic and context-dependent coping behaviours, rather than causally driven schemata of coping.

Furthermore, although in theory Lazarus' model allows for environmental feedback to alter the perceptions and, hence, perhaps to determine future coping in practice his taxonomy is rather static and emphasises coping styles, whilst tending to ignore coping behaviours (Dewe 1993) [65].

1.19 Coping as Problem Solving

Coping can also be viewed as a problem solving strategy (Cox, 1987) [66] has described a cycle of activities, beginning with recognition and diagnosis (analysis) followed by actions and evaluation through to reanalysis, which possibly represents the ideal problem-solving process. However, Schonpflug and Battmann (1988) [67] have emphasised that by adopting the wrong actions, or by failing, a person may create further problems and stress. At the same time, Meichenbaum (1977) [68] argues that 'catastrophizing' or reacting too strongly to such failure serves no adaptive purpose and it is often said that one of the few positive aspects to coping with stress is that the person learns from such experience.

However, Einhorn and Hogarth (1981) [69] suggest that there are at least three problems with this proposition: first, one does not necessarily know that there is something to be learned, second, what is to be learned is not clear, and third, there is ambiguity in judging whether one has learned. Furthermore, the problem solver may be fully occupied and not have any spare cognitive capacity for learning, and the emotion associated with stress may interfere with the learning process (Mandler, 1982) [70].

Coping may be seen as functional in its attempts to manage demands, either by changing them, redefining them (re-appraisal) or adapting to them. The styles and strategies used need to be relevant and applicable to the situation at hand. The choice and successful use of these responses will be determined by both the nature of the situation, by the personal and social resources available and also by the type of causal reasoning adopted in the appraisal process. Most contemporary theories of stress allow for individual differences in the experience of stress, and in how and how well it is coped with. Individual difference variables have been investigated as either: (1) components of the appraisal process, or (2) moderators of the stress-health relationship. Hence, researchers have asked, for example, to what extent are particular workers vulnerable to the experience of stress, or, for example, to what extent does, say, 'hardiness' moderate the relationship between job characteristics and worker health? This Report suggests that this distinction between individual differences as components of the appraisal process and moderators of the stress-outcome relationship can be easily understood in terms of transactional models of stress.

1.20 Prevention of Work Stress

There are a number of ways by which the risk of work stress can be reduced. These include:

Primary prevention, reducing stress through:

- Ergonomics.
- Work and environment design.
- Organisational and management development.

Secondary prevention, reducing stress through:

- Worker education and training.

Tertiary prevention, reducing the impact of stress by:

- Developing more sensitive and responsive management.
- Systems and enhanced occupational health provision.

The organisation itself is a generator of different types of risk. Tertiary prevention in organisations places an emphasis on the provision of responsive and efficient occupational health services. Contemporary work stress management should, therefore, encompass tertiary prevention. A good employer designs and manages work in a way avoids common risk factors for stress and prevents as much as possible foreseeable problems.

1.21 Three Ways of Dealing with Stress

There are few effective treatments that are easily fitted into a busy life style. In dealing with the stress different ways are as follows.

1. The relaxation response.
2. Managing emotions through Freeze-Frame.
3. Dealing with adrenaline addiction.

Relaxation Response: This treatment model has been developed by (Dr. Herbert Benson 1985) [71] and is widely described in his books. In many ways there is nothing new in this treatment model-religious people have been practicing the relaxation response or meditation for thousand of years. People with or without a personal faith can use the relaxation response and Herbert Benson suggests that clients use the following formant.

- Step One: Pick a brief phrase or word that reflects your basic belief system.
- Step Two: Choose a comfortable position.
- Step Three: Close your eyes.
- Step Four: Relax your muscles
- Step five: Become aware of your breathing, and start using your faith-rooted focus word.
- Step Six: Maintain a passive attitude.
- Step Seven: Continue for a set of period of time. Practice the technique for only ten to twenty minutes.
- Step Eight: Practice the technique twice daily.

This technique is easy. Nothing is required for us except trying to focus on a positive sentence or word. Many people are used to this. The Relaxation Response is built on this principle. We can recall that peace without being in the forest by focusing our eyes and mind on the experience. Dr. Benson's research shows that meditating on the walk is just as powerful in relaxation as actually being on it. This is very helpful in stress management. The only thing expected of the client is the willing to use 20 minutes a day focusing on a positive word or sentence.

There are many benefits from using this technique and they counteract some of the typical stress-related fight or flight response.

These results are very significant. Research shows (Paul Rosch, 1999) [72] that 1 in 6 people suffer chronic or severe recurrent headaches in the US. 90 percent of these headaches are classified as tension-type headaches, because of pain or the feeling of tightness of the muscles of the scalp and or neck. Dr. Paul Rosch in his article supports meditation as a traditional way to relieve the headaches. The chart above shows how muscle tension decreases by the use of the Relaxation Response. This is just one of the great advantages of using relaxation response.

This simple technique is non-addictive, costs nothing and can be exercised anywhere. It is also very cost-effective for employees in the organization or in the society. In his same article he mentions that headaches are responsible for more visits to the family doctor that any other complaint. But there are many other aspects of benefit that have been proved to be beneficial due to the use of relaxation response.

Relaxation Response can (Benson, 1984, p.119) [73]:

1. Break the anxiety cycle and relieve the anxiety-related symptoms of nausea, vomiting, diarrhoea, constipation and short-temperedness.
2. Combat attacks of hyperventilation.
3. Alleviate the pains of headache, backache and other pains such as angina pectoris.
4. Effectively treat many types of hypertension and heartbeat irregularities.
5. Alleviate insomnia.
6. Be utilized in the treatment of cancer.
7. Prevent the harmful effects of stress.
8. Be employed during exercise.
9. Enhance creativity.

Managing Emotions through Freeze-Frame

When we are under stress, it is suggested that we use what they have called Freeze-Frame Technique (Children, 1999 [74], p. 67).

1. Recognise the stressful feeling and Freeze-Frame it. Take a time-out.
2. Make sincere effort to shift your focus away from the racing mind or disturbed emotions to the area around your heart. Pretend you are breathing through your heart to help

focus your energy in this area. Keep your focus there for ten seconds or more.

3. Recall a positive, fun feeling or time you have had in life and try to re-experience it.
4. Now, using your intuition, commonsense, and sincerity, ask your heart: What would be a more efficient response to the situation, one that would minimize future stress?
5. Listen to what your heart says in answer to your question.

While the Relaxation Response is using concentration meditation as the main method, the Freeze-Frame is also looking for answers. When you Freeze-Frame or meditate, you influence your brain-waves, which is helpful. Under stress you experience high arousal adrenaline and your brain-waves help you to be effective. Dr. Archilbald Hart (1991 [75], p. 177) writes:

1. At low arousal, the brain waves are slow, bordering on drowsiness: they are called "theta" waves.
2. At medium arousal, the brain waves are typical of wakefulness and are called "alpha" waves.
3. At high arousal, the brain waves become faster and attention is highly focused. High arousal brain waves are called "beta" waves.

Yerkes–Dodson Law–Inverted–U:

1. At low arousal, we are not very effective in action tasks but very good at thinking creativity.
2. As arousal increases, we become more effective in action and less effective in creative thinking.
3. As arousal becomes very high, our efficiency in both action and thinking drops off again. This is probably the stage of panic.

By becoming drowsy we fall into a state of low arousal. "Theta" waves are triggered, and in this state the full power of memory is unlocked. With Freeze-Frame as part of relaxation the answer is while with the Relaxation Response you find peace of mind, and the answer comes out of this state. The HeartMath research centre has also researched what Freeze-

Frame is doing to the heart, pulse and respiration during Freeze-Frame. They concluded (McCraty, 2001 [76], p. 13):

"Our changing heart rhythms affect not only the heart but also the brain's ability to process information, including decision making, problem solving and creativity. They also directly affect how we feel."

Dr. Childre (1999) [77] concludes "when we use techniques like Freeze-Frame our heart rate variability, pulse transit time and respiration pattern are synchronised. This increases our efficiency, saving valuable energy and promotes health."

Dealing with Adrenaline Addiction: Dr. Archilbald hart is one of the key opponents to our society's addiction to adrenaline due to life style. He describes how a high level of adrenaline reduces our ability to rest, cuts down on our need to sleep and creates poor eating habits (Hart, 1991 [78], p. 7).

As part of stress response there is a release of adrenaline and noradrenaline which activates the heart muscle, increases cholesterol, sends glucose to muscles, raises blood pressure and increases the heart rate. This has serious consequences if it happens over an extended period of time.

- An increase in the production of blood cholesterol.
- A narrowing of the capillaries and other blood vessels that can shut down the blood supply to the heart muscle.
- A decrease in the body's ability to remove cholesterol.
- An increase in the blood's tendency to clot.
- An increase in the depositing of plaque on the walls of the arteries.

Hart describes some key features for "adrenaline addicts".

- They would rather engage in activity than sleep.
- Their activity helps them to forget their problems.
- Whenever they feel depressed, they turn to their activity to make them feel better.

Hart also describes some typical signs of adrenaline withdrawal. Here are some examples:

- A strong compulsion to be "doing something" while at

home or on vacation.

- A feeling of vague guilt while resting.
- Fidgetiness, restlessness, pacing, leg kicking, or fast gum chewing.
- An inability to concentrate for very long on any relaxing activity.
- Feelings of irritability and aggravation.

If this lifestyle continues, Hart concludes that: “The adrenaline system eventually ‘crashes’ and forces the victim into a state of prolonged and sever fatigue.” But this is not the only problem. Adrenaline also sets the stage for anxiety by influencing our brain’s biochemistry (Hart, 1999, p. 3). He states, “If the combination of your personality and work makes you an “adrenaline junkie”, you risk developing panic anxiety disorder”.

1.22 Managing Stress

Mangers of organizations have a dual perspective of stress. They need to be aware of their own stress levels, as well as those of their subordinates. Most of the literature focuses on ways of reducing stress. However, a more appropriate approach might be to examine ways of optimizing stress. French, Kast, and Rosenzweig (1985) [79] state that the challenge is to minimize distress and maintain eustress. They point out that the conditions of organizational life create a series of paradoxes that demonstrate the need for balance and equilibrium.

1. Uncertainty can lead to distress, but so can certainties or over control.
2. Pressure can lead to distress, but so can limbo or lack of contact.
3. Responsibility can lead to distress, but so can lack of responsibility or insignificance.
4. Performance evaluation can lead to distress, but so can lack of feedback concerning performance.
5. Role ambiguity can lead to distress, but so can job

descriptions that constrain individuality (p. 708).

The role of management becomes one of maintaining an appropriate level of stress by providing an optimal environment, and "by doing a good job in areas such as performance planning, role analysis, work redesign/job enrichment, continuing feedback, ecological considerations, and interpersonal skills training" (p. 709).

There are essentially three strategies for dealing with stress in organizations (Jick and Payne, 1980) [80]: 1) treat the symptoms, 2) change the person, and 3) remove the cause of the stress. When a person is already suffering from the effects of stress, the first priority is to treat the symptoms. This includes both the identification of those suffering from excessive stress, as well as providing health-care and psychological counselling services. The second approach is to help individuals build stress management skills to make them less vulnerable to its effects. Examples would be teaching employees' time management and relaxation techniques, or suggesting changes to one's diet or exercise. The third approach is to eliminate or reduce the environmental situation that is creating the stress. This would involve reducing environmental stressors such as noise and pollution, or modifying production schedules and work-loads.

Many modern organizations view the management of stress as a personal matter. An effort to monitor employee stress levels would be considered an invasion of privacy. However, Lawless (1991) [81] found that nine out of ten employees felt that it was the employers responsibility to reduce worker stress and provide a health plan that covers stress illnesses. She emphasized that "employees have no doubt that stress-related illnesses and disability should be taken seriously. Employees expect substantive action by their employer and hold their employer financially responsible for the consequences of job stress" (p. 12).

Lawless (1991) [82] reported that four different employer programs were effective in reducing job burn out, where the percent of people reporting burn out was reduced by half. Furthermore, when these programs were offered, there were also half as many stress related illnesses. They are: (1) supportive work and family policies, (2) effective management communication, (3) health insurance coverage for mental illness and chemical dependency, and (4) flexible scheduling of work hours. This study also reported that the success rate for treating stress related disabilities was considerably less than the average for all disabilities, and that the average cost to treat stress related conditions was US$ 1,925 (both successful and unsuccessful).

Managers can take active steps to minimize undesirable stress in themselves and their subordinates. Williams and Huber (1986) [83] suggest five managerial actions that can be used to reduce stress in workers.

1. Clarifying task assignments, responsibility, authority, and criteria for performance evaluation.
2. Introducing consideration for people into one's leadership style.
3. Delegating more effectively and increasing individual autonomy where the situation warrants it.
4. Clarifying goals and decision criteria.
5. Setting and enforcing policies for mandatory vacations and reasonable working hours (p. 252).

Establishing one's priorities (i.e., value clarification) is an important step in the reduction of stress. The demands of many managerial positions cause the neglect of other areas of one's life, such as family, friends, recreation, and religion. This neglect creates stress, which in turn affects job performance and health. Value clarification is linked to time management, since we generally allocate our time according to our priorities. By setting personal priorities, managers and subordinates can reduce this source of stress. It is typically the first step in any stress reduction program.

Many sources of stress in organizations cannot be changed. These might include situations like a prolonged recessionary period, new competitors, or an unanticipated crisis. Organizational members generally have little control over these kinds of stressors, and they can create extended periods of high-stress situations. People who adjust to these stressors generally use a form of perceptual adaptation, where they modify the way in which they perceive the situation.

Other sources of stress in organizations can be changed. One particularly effective way for managers to minimize employee stress is to clarify ambiguities, such as job assignments and responsibilities. (Arnold and Feldman, 1986) [84] Employee stress is directly related to the amount of uncertainty in their tasks, expectations, and roles. Managers can encourage employees to search for more information when they are given unfamiliar tasks, or when they are uncertain of their roles. Another way to reduce employee stress is to incorporate time management techniques, as well as setting realistic time schedules for the completion of projects.

There are many other successful ways of dealing with stress. These include stress reduction workshops, tranquilizers, biofeedback, meditation, self-hypnosis, and a variety of other techniques designed to relax an individual. Programs that teach tolerance for ambiguity often report positive effects. One of the most promising is a health maintenance program that stresses the necessity of proper diet, exercise and sleep. Social support systems seem to be extremely effective in preventing or relieving the deleterious effects of stress. Friends and family can provide a nurturing environment that builds self-esteem, and makes one less susceptible to stress. One study found that government white-collar workers who received support from their supervisors, peers, and subordinates experienced fewer physical symptoms of stress. (Katz and Kahn, 1978) [85] Managers can create nurturing and supportive environments to help minimize job-related stress.

Albrecht (1979) [86] hypothesized that there are eight relatively "universal" factors that come into play when evaluating the balance between stress and reward (job satisfaction) in organizations. These are: (1) workload, (2) physical variables, (3) job status, (4) accountability, (5) task variety, (6) human contact, (7) physical challenge, and (8) mental challenge. Each individual has a "comfort zone" for the eight factors. The goal of management is to find the "comfort zone" for each employee that results in optimal performance without producing undesirable side effects. Albrecht's taxonomy is important because it recognizes the necessity of balance. For example, Taylorism stresses the ideas of maximum output, minimal task variety, and continuous supervision. The predicted effect of these imbalances would be stress and a reduction in job satisfaction. Perhaps many of today's organizational problems with worker stress are the result of the effective application of Taylorism.

The social climate of an organization is often viewed as a cause of stress. However, social climate is a relativistic concept, and "the social climate of an organization is whatever most of the people think it is" (Albrecht, 1979 [87], p. 167). There are three factors that need to be examined when evaluating social climate. The first is the degree to which employees identify with or alienate themselves from the organization. Employee attitude surveys are an effective method of measuring this factor. Identification can be measured through employees pride in membership, and the extent to which they take initiative and offer constructive suggestions.

Alienation can be detected by examining whether members openly criticize the organization, or the degree to which they oppose change. The second factor of organizational climate is the degree to which labour and management are polarized. One of the most effective ways of dealing with this problem is to make all levels of management more visible and accessible. Employees are less likely to criticize management who they see on a regular basis. The goal is to change to perception from "they" (the managers) to "we" (the members of the organization). The third factor is the perceived social norms of the organization. Social norms are abstract organizational values, such as trust, fairness, and respect. Interviews and questionnaires can be used to ascertain organizational social norms, but corrective action involves setting up management programs that clarify organizational values, and may involve replacing certain managers when necessary.

Quick and Quick (1984) [88] suggest several diagnostic procedures for determining stress levels in organizations. Interviews allow in-depth probing, but they are time consuming and depend primarily on the listening skills of the interviewer. Questionnaires have the advantage of being able to process higher volumes of data, but they often lose the "flavour" or feel of the responses. Observational techniques (both medical and behavioural) can be either quantitative or qualitative. Quantitative techniques might involve gathering company records, such as the rates of absenteeism, tardiness, turnover, and production. Qualitative techniques involve observing workers for signs of stress-related behaviour.

Job engineering and job redesign are recent concepts that attempt to minimize job-related stress. Job engineering takes into account the values and needs of the worker, as well as the production objectives of the organization (Albrecht, 1979). [89] It involves a six-step cyclical process, beginning with defining the job objectives. This initial step makes statements about "accomplishing something of recognized value" (p. 159). The second step is to define the job conditions. This step specifies the physical, social, and psychological characteristics of the job. The third step is to define the job processes, equipment, and materials. Processes are often presented in a flow chart to show the sequence of operations. The fourth step is to re-evaluate the design from the perspective of the worker, the goal being to achieve a balance between job satisfaction and performance. The fifth step is to test the job design. Employees often experience problems not anticipated by job engineers. The evaluation should look at the "total combination of person, equipment, materials, processes, and surroundings as an integrated whole, and you must measure both productivity and employee satisfaction before you can say the job is well designed" (p. 162) the sixth step involves the ongoing re-evaluation and redesign of the job. Employee attitudes and values change, and new technology provide alternatives to the status quo. Job engineering attempts to be sensitive to these changes, and to modify job descriptions is necessary.

Sevelius (1986) [90] describes his experience implementing a wellness education program at a large manufacturing plant. Several successful techniques were used. Booklets on specific health subjects were place in "Take one" bins conveniently located around the plant. The booklets were positively received and increased employee's awareness and knowledge. Campaigns were undertaken to highlight the specific themes in the booklets. Group lectures were tried and found to be ineffective because less than ten percent of the employees attended them. In addition, the lectures were video taped, but employees did not take the time to view them. Medical examinations generally did not reveal hidden illnesses, however, they were found to be of considerable value because they gave employees the opportunity of individual medical counselling. Sevelius suggests that peer support systems might also be successful in the workplace.

Notes

1. Selye, H., "History of the Stress Concept," in L. Goldberger and S. Breznitz, eds., *The Handbook of Stress,* 2nd edition, New York: The Free Press, 1993.
2. World Health Organization [WHO] (1986) Constitution of the World Health Organization. In: Basic Documents (36th ed.). World Health Organization, Geneva. Ibid.
3. Dewe, P., Leiter, M and Cox, T. (eds.) (2000) Coping, Health and Organisations. London: Taylor and Francis.
4. Griffiths, A.J. (1999a) Work design and management-The older worker. Experimental Aging Research, 25 (4), pp.411-420.
5. Ilmarinen J., and Rantanen J. (1999) Promotion of work ability

during ageing. American Journal of Industrial Medicine, No. S1, pp. 21-23.

6. Lazarus, R.S., and Folkman, S.(1984). Stress, appraisal and coping. New York: Springer Publishing Co.
7. McGrath, J. E. 1976. "Stress and behaviour in organizations." In *Handbook of Industrial and Organizational Psychology.* Dunnett, M.D. (ed.) Chicago: Rand McNally College Publishing. : McGraw Hill.
8. Arnold, H.J., and Feldman. 1986. *Organizational Behaviour.* New York Lazarus, R.S., and Folkman, S. (1984). Stress, appraisal and coping. New York: Springer Publishing Co.
9. Williams, J.C., and Huber, G.P. 1986. *Human Behaviour in Organizations.* Cincinnati, OH: South-Western Publishing.
10. Perls, F. S., 1969. *Gestalt Therapy Verbatim.* Lafayette, CA: Real People Press.
11. French, W.L.., Kast, F.E., and Rosenzweig, J.E. 1985. *Understanding Human Behaviour in Organizations.* New York: Harper and Row.
12. Selye, H., *The Stress of Life,* New York: McGraw-Hill, 1956.
13. Mandler, G., "Thought, Memory, and Learning: Effects of Emotional Stress," in L. Goldberger and S. Breznitz, eds., *The Handbook of Stress,* 2nd edition, New York: The Free Press, 1993.
14. Cox, T. (1978) Stress. Macmillan, London.
15. Cox, T. (1990) The recognition and measurement of stress: conceptual and methodological issues. In: E.N. Corlett and J. Wilson (eds.) Evaluation of Human Work. Taylor and Francis, London.
16. Fletcher, B.C. (1988) The epidemiology of occupational stress. In: C.L. Cooper and R. Payne (eds.) Causes, Coping and Consequences of Stress at Work. Wiley and Sons, Chichester.
17. Spielberger, C.D. (1976) The nature and measurement of anxiety. In C.D. Spielberger and R. Diaz-Guerrero (eds.) Cross-Cultural Anxiety. Hemisphere, Washington DC. Spielberger, C.D. (1976) The nature and measurement of anxiety. In C.D. Spielberger and R. Diaz-Guerrero (eds.) Cross-Cultural Anxiety. Hemisphere, Washington DC.
18. Sutherland, V.J., and Cooper, CL (1990) Understanding stress: psychological perspective for health professionals. Psychology and Health, series: 5. Chapman and Hall, London.

19. Selye, H. (1950) Stress, Acta Incorporated, Montreal.
20. Ibid.
21. Cox, T. (1985a) The nature and measurement of stress. Ergonomics, 28, pp. 1155-1163.
22. Ibid.
23. Ibid.
24. Scheuch, K. (1996): Stress and resources at work in a changing society. Bremerhaven: Wirtschaftsverlag NW, pp. 95-109 (Schriftenreihe der Bundesanstalt für Arbeitsmedizin: Tagungsbericht 11).
25. Scheuch, K. (1990): Psychosoziale Faktoren im Arbeitsprozeß und Gesundheit: Einführung. Z. ges. Hyg. 36, 403-407.
26. Ibid.
27. International Labour Organization [ILO] (1986) Psychosocial Factors at Work: Recognition and Control. Occupational Safety and Health Series no: 56, International Labour Office, Geneva.
28. World Health Organization [WHO] (1986) Constitution of the World Health Organization. In: Basic Documents (36th ed.). World Health Organization, Geneva.
29. Cox, T., and Cox, S. (1993) Psychosocial and Organizational Hazards: Monitoring and Control. Occasional Series in Occupational Health, No. 5. World Health Organization (Europe), Copenhagen, Denmark.
30. Cox, T. and Griffiths, A.J. (1995) The assessment of psychosocial hazards at work. In M.J. Shabracq, J.A.M. Winnubst and C.L. Cooper (eds.) Handbook of Work and Health Psychology. Chichester: Wiley and Sons.
31. Ibid.
32. Bammer, K., and Newberry, B.H. (1983). Stress and Cancer. Toronto: C.J. Hogrefe.
33. Ibid.
34. Allen, R.J. (1983). Human Stress: Its nature and Control. Minneapolis, MN: Burgess Publishing Company.
35. Bhagat, R. S. 1983. "Effects of stressful life events on individual performance effectiveness and work adjustment processes within organizational settings: A research model." *Academy of Management Review*. 8(4): 660-671.
36. Albrecht, K. 1979. *Stress and the Manager*. Englewood Cliffs, NJ: Prentice-Hall.
37. French, W.L.., Kast, F.E., and Rosenzweig, J.E. 1985.

Understanding Human Behaviour in Organizations. New York: Harper and Row.

38. Parasuraman, S., and Alutto, J.A. 1984. "Sources and outcomes of stress in organizational settings: Toward the development of a structural model." *Academy of Management Journal* 27: 330-350.
39. Ibid.
40. Friedman, M., and Rosenman, R. 1974. *Type A Behaviour and Your Heart*. New York: Knopf.
41. Matthews, K. A. 1982. "Psychological perspectives on the Type A behaviour pattern." *Psychological Bulletin* 91: 293-323.
42. Organ, D. W. 1979. "The meaning of stress." *Business Horizons* 6: 32-40.
43. Friedman, M., & Rosenman, R.H.(1974). Type A Behaviour and Your Heart. Connecticut: A Fawcett Crest Book.
44. Goodheart, Annette (1994). Laughter Therapy. Santa Barbara. Less Stress Press.
45. Selye, H. (1956) Stress of Life. McGraw-Hill, New York.
46. Yerkes, R., and J. Dodson, "The Relation of Strength of Stimulus to Rapidity of Habit Formation," Journal of Comparative Neurology and Psychology, Vol. 18, 1908, pp. 459-482.
47. Selye, H. (1936) A syndrome produced by diverse nocuous agents. Nature, 138, 32.
48. Hart, Archibald D. (1999). The Anxiety Cure. Nashville: Word.
49. Hart, Arachibald D. (1991). The Hidden Link Between Adrenalin and Stress. Dallas: Word.
50. Dewe, P. (1993) Work, stress and coping: common pathways for future research? Work and Stress, 7(1), 1-3.
51. Dewe, P. (2000) Measures of coping with stress at work: a review and critique. In P. Dewe, M. eiter and T. Cox (eds.) Coping, Health and Organisations. London: Taylor and Francis.
52. Lazarus, R.S. (1966) Psychological Stress and the Coping Process. McGraw-Hill, New York.
53. Folkman, S. (1984). Personal control and stress and coping processes: a theoretical analysis. Journal of Personality and Social Psychology, 46, 839-852.
54. Lazarus, R.S. and Folkman, S. (1984). Stress, Appraisal and Coping. Springer Publications, New York.
55. Ibid.

56. Ibid.
57. Ibid.
58. Ibid.
59. Dewe, P. (1987) New Zealand ministers of religion: identifying sources of stress and coping strategies. Work and Stress, 1, 351-363.
60. Pearlin, L., and Schooler, C. (1978). The structure of coping. Journal of Health and Social Behaviour, 19, 2-21.
61. Pearlin, L., Lieberman, M.L., Menaghan, E., and Mullan, J.T. (1981) The stress process. Journal of Health and Social Behaviour, 19, 2 - 21.
62. Miller, S. (1979). Controllability and human stress: method, evidence and theory. Behavioural Research and Therapy, 17, 28-304.
63. Salo, K. (1995) Teacher stress and coping over an autumn term in Finland. Work and Stress, 9 (1), 55-66.
64. Wykes, J. and Whittington, R. (1991) Coping strategies used by staff following assault by a patient: an exploratory study. Work and Stress, 5 (1), 37-48.
65. Dewe, P. (1993) Work, stress and coping: common pathways for future research? Work and Stress, 7 (1), 1-3.
66. Cox, T. (1987). Stress, coping and problem solving. Work and Stress, 1, 5-14.
67. Schonpflug, F. and Battmann, A. (1988) The costs and benefits of coping. In: S. Fisher & J. Reason (eds.) Handbook of Life Stress, Cognition and Health. Wiley & Son, Chichester.
68. Meichenbaum, D. (1977) Cognitive-Behaviour Modification. Plenum Press, New York.
69. Einhorn, H.J., and Hogarth, R.M. (1981) Behavioural decision theory: processes of judgement and choice. Annual Review of Psychology, 32, 53-88.
70. Mandler, G. (1982) Stress and thought processes. In: L. Goldberg and S. Breznitz (eds.) Handbook of Stress: Theoretical and Clinical Aspects. Free Press, New York.
71. Benson, Herbert 1985. Beyond the Relaxation Response. New York: Berkley Books.
72. Rosch, Paul (1999). Stress, Headache, and other Head Pain. Health and Stress, 3, 1-8.
73. Ibid.
74. Childre, D., and Martin, H. (1999). The Heartmath Solution, San

Francisco: Hyper San Francisco.

75. Ibid.
76. McCraty, R, Atkinsson, M., and Tomasino, D. (2001). Science of the Heart. CA: Institute of Heartmath.
77. Ibid.
78. Ibid.
79. Ibid.
80. *Journal* 5: 50-55.Jick, T.D., and Payne, R. 1980. "Stress at work." *Exchange: The Organizational Behavioural Teaching Journal* 5: 50-55.
81. Ibid.
82. Ibid.
83. Ibid.
84. Ibid.
85. Ibid.
86. Albrecht, K. 1979. *Stress and the Manager*. Englewood Cliffs, NJ: Prentice-Hall.
87. Ibid.
88. Quick, J.C., and Quick, J.D. 1984. *Organizational Stress and Preventive Management*. New York: McGraw-Hill.
89. Ibid.
90. Sevelius, G. 1986. "Experience with preventative measures." In *Occupational Stress*. Wolf, S. G., Jr. and Finerstone, A. J. (eds.) pp. 191-211. Littleton, MA: PSG Publishing.

2

Total Quality Management Techniques

2.1 What is Total Quality Management?

A primary role of management is to lead an organization in its day-to-day operations as well as to maintain it as a viable entity into the future. Quality has become an important factor to succeed in this latter strategic responsibility. Total Quality is a description of the culture, attitude and organization of a company that strives to provide customers with products and services that satisfy their needs. The culture requires quality in all aspects of the company's operations, with processes being done and defects and the defects are controlled. Total Quality Management (TQM) is a method by which management and employees can become involved in the continuous improvement of the production of goods and services. It is a combination of quality and management tools aimed at increasing business and reducing losses due to irrelevant practices. Some of the companies which have implemented TQM include Ford Motor Company, Phillips Semiconductor, SGL Carbon, Motorola and Toyota Motor Company.

Life long, learning is a process that can be done in almost every scene of life. Work place is one good platform to learn continuously. At work, one can learn how to accomplish certain tasks, how to behave in making decisions, how to treat other people within the organization, and how to cope with the everlasting changes. Hayes (1997) [1] stated that if a company is to develop the ability of continuous self-renewal, it's real battle lies in changing individual organisation members' behaviours and actions. In the late 1980s, providing customer satisfaction in customer terms became a specific goal of business organisation. Providing high quality was recognized as a key element for success. At the end of the twentieth century, business organizations were involved in what has become a quality revolution. It began in Japan and has spread to other parts of the world. It involves an entirely new way of thinking about and dealing with quality that encompasses the organisation. This new approach has been given a variety of names viz., "Six Sigma" at Motorola, "Leadership through Quality" at Xerox, "Perfect Design Quality" at Intel and "Total Quality Control" at Hewlett-Packard, but more often referred to as "Total Quality Management".

Organisations everywhere are growing increasingly conscious of the competitive potential quality. Quality has become an issue because standards are now specifically defined whereas previously they were vague and unmonitored. Competition focuses not only on price but quality. In the present economic and political climate, even higher standards are demanded in the face of diminishing resources. In the early 1900s, F.W. Taylor, the 'Father of Scientific Management', emphasized on quality by including product inspection and gauging in his list of fundamental areas of manufacturing management.

2.2 Origin of TQM

The concept of "total quality" evolved in US in the 1970s and consists of a people focused management system that aims at continued increase in customer satisfaction. It involves all employees, executives and top management personnel and extend backward and forward to include the supply chain and the customer chain. "Total Quality Management (TQM) is a philosophy that involves everyone in an organisation in a continual effort to improve quality and achieve customer." There are two key philosophies in TQM. One is a never-ending push to improve (i.e. continuous improvement or kaizen in Japanese) and the other is a goal of customer satisfaction, which involves meeting or exceeding customer expectations.

TQM is a management philosophy that seeks to integrate

all organizational functions (marketing, finance, design, engineering, and production, customer service, etc.) to focus on meeting customer needs and organizational objectives. Total quality management (TQM) denotes the system of managing for total quality. TQM is a total, Company wide effort through full involvement of the entire work force with a focus on continuous improvement to achieve maximum possible customer satisfaction. Total quality control, which is the previous step to TQM, is an effective system for integrating the quality development, Quality maintenance and quality improvement efforts of the various groups in an organisation to achieve highest productivity and customer satisfaction.

TQM views an organization as a collection of processes. It maintains that organizations must strive to continuously improve these processes by incorporating the knowledge and experiences of workers. The simple objective of TQM is "Do the right things, right the first time, every time". TQM is infinitely variable and adaptable. Although originally applied to manufacturing operations, and for a number of years only used in that area, TQM is now becoming recognized as a generic management tool, just as applicable in service and public sector organizations. There are a number of evolutionary strands, with different sectors creating their own versions from the common ancestor. TQM is the foundation for activities, which include:

- Commitment by senior management and all employees,
- Meeting customer requirements,
- Reducing development cycle times,
- Just in Time/Demand Flow Manufacturing,
- Improvement teams,
- Challenging quantified goals and benchmarking,
- Reducing product and service costs,
- Systems to facilitate improvement,
- Line Management ownership,
- Employee involvement and empowerment,

- Recognition and celebration,
- Focus on processes/improvement plans, and
- Specific incorporation in strategic planning.

To understand this we have to look into the history. At the beginning of the 20th century, industrial progress was mostly restricted to European countries and the U.S.A. other countries were not making any significant progress. But, during the last fifty years, industrialization and associated technical innovations have made mind-boggling progress. Now, except for a few countries almost all are vying for a place in the fierce global market trade. Morris Foster and Susan whittle in their article "the quality management maze" reviewed the development of TQM. In attempting to reduce some of the confusion, which arose from ill defined and inconsistent terms of quality control and quality management, they remarkably classified quality management in to four phases.

Quality Control (QC) Phase: QC focuses on product defect detection through postproduction inspection. It is concerned with the adherence to standards and sorting out rejects.

Quality Assurance (QA) Phase: QA recognizes that "inspection is not the answer" and that "the entire manufacturing process must be committed to meeting the quality needs of the design". QA focuses on procedure compliance and product conformity to specifications through production and operations management, often using statistical process control (SPC) as "tracking" tool.

Total Quality Control (TQC) Phase: TQC programmers attempt to expand the QA philosophy beyond manufacturing operations in to other areas of organizational life. TQC incorporates many of the tools used in QA, but the purpose of problem analysis is developing long-term solutions rather than responds to short-term variations. Concerns with direct cost reduction and a preoccupation with efficiency or ousted in favour of the pursuit of quality through the elimination waste and non-value added procedures and assuring continues improvement through the refinement and expansion of quality control systems and procedures. The utilization of computer integrated manufacturing systems and just-in-time operations management methods also facilitate this control. Management of the manufacturing system then extends outside the factory gate to tie-in suppliers, distributors and customers in the "chain of quality". But problems have arisen in the adoption, as TQC is supposed to be a company-wide moment but actually is largely limited to the manufacturing department.

Total Quality Management (TQM) Phase: TQM is a fundamental shift from what has gone before. The systematic analysis, preplanning and blue printing of operations remains essential, but the focus switches from a process driven by external controls through procedure compliance and enhancement to a process of habitual improvement. Where control is embedded within and is driven by the culture of the organisation. Senior management's role is to provide leadership and support. In TQM, customer orientation achieved through continuous quality improvement becomes a valid "taken for granted" atmosphere shared by everyone, unquestioned and habitually enacted. As the atmosphere is increasingly taken for granted by everyone, it becomes non-debatable and drops out of awareness to be embedded in the organisation culture.

One of the first things that Deming (1982) [2] taught in exercising TQM is adopting the new philosophy, realizing that today is the new economic age. Commonly accepted levels of delays, mistakes, defective materials, and defective workmanship are no longer tolerable. This awareness should be the beginning of the TQM learning process. In exercising Total Quality Management, all employees should not only have information on what TQM is, but also gain knowledge, the know-what, know-why, know-how, and know-who of TQM. Before the practices of TQM in the 1970s, Japanese products were considered products of lower quality in the world market. In Japan, where people are taught to work hard to survive, this new philosophy might be easier to absorb under the shadow of Japan's huge loss in the Second World War, and the motivation to excel in the world market. Looking at the success gained by the Japanese firms implementing TQM, US firms were beginning to adopt this "new" practice.

Knowledge as the Commodity in Learning to Know Knowledge is a deeper concept than information. The term 'knowledge' itself is arguable. Barnett (2000) [3] noted that in western tradition knowledge has come to stand for ordered conceptual frameworks, providing systematic holds on the world, expressed in written and spoken language. The idea of knowledge contains elements of universality. Meanwhile, Peat (1995) [4] described that knowledge can be seen as information that comes with insights, framed experience, intuition, judgment, and values, thus contain locality. Traditional cultures represent a different form of knowledge expressed in written or spoken language, and consciously or unconsciously, traditional people educate their children how to live in traditional life. People all over the world learn formally and informally.

In some sense knowledge represents truth and therefore offers a reliable basis for action. Clarke and Rollo (2001) [5] refer knowledge as the body of understanding and skills that is mentally constructed by people. Knowledge is increased through interaction with information typically from other people. Business organisations are coming to the view that knowledge is their most valuable strategic resource. They are realising that in order to remain competitive they must explicitly manage their intellectual resources and capabilities embedded in knowledge. Intuitively, it makes sense that the firm that knows more about its customers, products, technologies and markets, and their linkages should perform better (Zack, 1999). [6]

These arguments are in alliance with the idea of autopsies (Barnett, 2000) [7] that implies that company-specific processes can count as knowledge. TQM as a system encourages people in the organization to acknowledge their environment specifically and communicate the information effectively. In implementing TQM, each member of the organization learns to know their customers, suppliers, all stakeholders, and other specific information altogether. These types of information are considered as company-specific knowledge that enables TQM optimising the company's value.

2.3 How to Learn to Know?

In initiating TQM, all levels employees would be trained on 'quality' courses and trainings. In this early stage, the process of learning to know is usually formal as classes are formed and formal instructors are assigned to share the total quality knowledge. Transfer of knowledge is mostly limited to mere theoretical knowledge. Knowledge is of no Use without Implementation Thomas Clarke (2001) [8] argued that knowledge management initiatives are unlikely to be successful unless they are integrated with business strategy, and related to the development of the core capabilities of the organisation. Similar claim noted by Barnett (2000) [9], knowledge is only authentic if it can be put to work. Therefore, the 'learning to know' pillar only is not enough in exercising TQM. The four pillars of life long learning (learning to know, do, be, and live together) should be built in TQM.

2.4 Learning to Do

Wisdom could be described as the best use of knowledge (Clarke, Rollo, 2001). [10] Knowledge processes can always be improved but wisdom is necessary to determine which processes to focus on in order to achieve organisational objectives. After the members learn to know what TQM is, they have to learn how to do and implement it in the work place wisely. From Skill to Competence, Top Management Commitment Skill only is not enough in the TQM process. All members should excel in their very own vicinity. The goal of all TQM members should be creating competence. Top management and the shareholders should commit to the TQM application and the ultimate goal, producing competence, not skill.

Once the management and the shareholders were committed to implement TQM, they have to communicate clearly this new direction to all employees and to make sure that everyone within the company understands the TQM strategies thoroughly and acquires competence, not merely the skill. Peterson (1999) [11] affirmed, top management must have a passion for TQM application. Without this sustained passion, top management's attention and energy would be diverted to other pressing needs.

In this 'learning to do' process, senior members teach juniors how to gain competence in TQM. As Kotter (1996) [12] stated, successful implementation occurs in companies where executives 'walk the talk', teaching new behaviours by example. The determinant of success of enterprises is ever more reliant upon their effectiveness in gathering and utilising knowledge, that is, their competence. In exercising TQM, companies require good coordination of complex activities, such as manufacturing and procurement, and therefore competent employees are needed to operate the system. Top management role in demonstrating examples is the key to gain competence among TQM members.

More informal learning instigates more tacit knowledge transferred in implementing TQM, companies develop formal organized learning support, such as quality circles, mentoring, visits, and formal educational trainings. In TQM, quality circles as formal small groups are scheduled to meet in a regular basis to talk about problems, evaluations, and other things involving quality. These groups might work in certain cultures as Japan and other Asian countries. However, it may not work that well in western world. Eraut (1998) [13] found in their research conducted in the United Kingdom that informal mentoring and coaching would be more effective rather than formal ones. The more formal the meeting, the less tacit knowledge transferred. Argyris (1994) [14] of Harvard University also stated that correctly used communication tools such as focus groups actually inhibit the learning and communication that corporations now demand of managers and employees.

Those formal communication tools do not encourage individual accountability or allow the revelation of threatening or embarrassing information. Tacit knowledge is important to spread among all TQM members as they not only have to gain skills, but also competence. Therefore, quality circles in TQM should be not too formal and gradually develop interpersonal support which might extend beyond workplace. In Japan, after office hour people usually gather at pubs, mainly to drink and talk and this would strengthen their personal and social relationships as well as at work as members of TQM team. The formal quality circles at work become more informal for them as they are bound by personal friendship.

Hence, the transfer of tacit knowledge would be less difficult. This is not the case in the west where people value individualism more. The disappointment of TQM in western world might due to these arguments. The ways Americans and Japanese learn to do are dissimilar. With the Japanese frame of reference, where security is the most important concern, they are more willing to learn to do their best in performing quality. Defect could mean the termination of wealth leading to death. Consequently, zero-defect is understandable among Japanese workers. They would learn to do the TQM with a clear goal of achieving prime quality, for it is their way to survive. The American frame of reference assesses pride and self-actualization the highest. Americans would tend to seek pleasure on top of work. The zero-defect concept would be considered 'not human.' They would learn to implement TQM as another type of a Japanese worth-trying management method. Therefore, cultural background could be a moderating factor in learning to do the TQM.

2.5 Learning to Be

Knowledge produced by individuals reaches its full potential to create economic value when it becomes embedded in organisational routines. It is important to focus upon flows of knowledge, and not simply measure stocks of knowledge (Clarke and Rollo, 2001). [15] It is implied that the results of the learning processes can be observed in how the learners become the features they have learned. To Be the Members of TQM All members should learn to be part of the whole total quality management team. In TQM, there is no useless member. Every one is useful, every one is important.

It is obvious that Deming stated the characteristics of the TQM members as an important requirement in contributing success to TQM. The workers and management team in the TQM are required to 'be' true members with certain characteristics, not merely to work and be able to do things. Some companies create certain specific features distinguishing the company's TQM members from other companies to build the sense of pride and sense of belonging. The management constantly imposes total quality character building on workers as TQM can only be success when supported by well-built total quality characters of the team.

TQM is not just a method that can be learned, but the implementation needs to be nurtured every day to build positive attitudes towards the success of maximizing quality. The people within the organization should learn how to be supportive members of the TQM. Building a community of TQM is the hardest part of implementing TQM. Community-shared understanding and access to the work and minds of others-is the principal element in an innovation strategy (Compaq, 1999). [16] Being knowledge-able of TQM does not only mean understanding all the information about TQM. It covers the 518 institutionalization of the new behaviours, values and attitudes into the organization's shared values and belief system on TQM. All members of the organization now are exposed to TQM and gain knowledge on how to utilize it for the purpose of the company's goal achievements, maximizing quality.

The TQM members have their trademark as TQM members. While Deming (1982) [17] insisted that there was no 'instant pudding' in implementing TQM, many western consultants are establishing themselves with a client suggested short-term gains. Because of this search for short-term gains, process improvement and reductions in cycle time became very popular and in some cases a final objective. Unfortunately, after they ran their short-term course, many efforts collapsed and TQM was often declared a failure. In these cases, the so-called 'TQM members' are not really TQM members. They do not acquire the attitudes and characteristics of TQM members as Deming pointed. More informal learning involves in shaping the members to gain all the attitudes and characteristics of TQM members and this takes time.

2.6 Continuous Improvement as a Life Style

TQM is a long-term process and it involves continuous improvement. It requires the change of attitudes of the employees. One very important characteristic required in TQM is the ability to improve continuously. This characteristic comes from the willingness to improve, to be the best. Therefore a very high standard should be set in order to push TQM members to continuously improve. In the east, usually children are taught to fight for their goals at any cost and not to be easily satisfied. This character is nurtured from early age. The zero-defect requirement in TQM would be easily implemented where people are used to have the highest standards and continuously fight toward them. When the zero-defect was first introduced to the western world, it was quite shocking as western people are usually more tolerant. In the west, to err is human and this philosophy certainly does not fit the TQM philosophy. In implementing TQM, all members should learn to have a TQM life style.

Argyris (1991) [18] argued that (western) professionals are

least able to learn because they have rarely experienced learning-related failure and are prone to defensive reasoning. This perhaps could be one of the biggest hindrances in implementing TQM in established industrial world, as professionals unconsciously are not willing to change their lifestyle and habit to some new things. Total Quality Management is a lifestyle. It is not merely a system of management. It involves all aspects of the employees' and management's life. Japan today has adopted this prime quality life-style in all aspects of their life.

2.7 Loyalty and High Expectation as TQM Life Style

Lincoln (1989) [19] compared employee work attitudes and management practice in the US and Japan. The research results showed that with the causal reciprocity thus statistically controlled, satisfaction in Japan is lower but commitment and loyalty to the company proved substantially higher than in the US. The resulting picture of Japanese work attitudes as combining low job satisfaction and high organizational commitment might be an evidence that the discipline of the Japanese work force does have some basis in the work attitudes of Japanese employees.

With high commitment and loyalty, the Japanese would employ continuous improvement naturally. This might explain the early successful implementation of total quality management as life long learning at work place in Japanese firms. Japanese employee's combination of high commitment couples with low satisfaction may imply a restless striving for perfection, an ongoing quest for fulfilment of lofty work values and company goals. High percentages of the US workforce routinely reporting satisfaction with their jobs may be more cause for concern than complacency. It may signal low expectations and aspirations, and a preoccupation with leisure-time pursuits.

Another possibility is that the Japan-US differences in work attitude found are due to measurement biases. Many would argue that a distinctly American impulse is to put the best face on things, to be upbeat and cheerful, to appear in control and successful even when uncertainty is high and the future looks bleak. The Japanese, it appears, bias their assessments in the opposite direction. The Japanese seem to colour their evaluations of nearly everything with a large dose of pessimism, humility, and understatement. A Japanese child coming home from school with a B for a test might get scolded for being 'failed' to get an A. An American child in the same condition might get rewarded for his achievement. It is arguable that the Japanese would have a stronger coerce to learn life-long, since their expectation is higher than the average Americans.

In TQM, high expectation combined with high loyalty is very important in creating prime quality. Scott et al. (1999) [20] showed an example experienced by General Motors, a prominent American firm which has saved millions of dollars by going to a just-in-time system. While 519 implementing TQM, if there is a breakdown in the supply of inventory to the system, the result can be catastrophic. In 1996 GM was hit by a strike that involved about 3,000 workers at two of its plants that produces brakes for the cars GM makes. As a result of not having brakes for the cars to put in cars, GM was forced to stop production and lay-off over 177,000 workers. Moreover, because GM used a just-in-time inventory system, it did not take long for the shutdown of the brake plant to affect all of GM's other operations.

In Japan, this kind of strike among TQM members would hardly happen for TQM is their life-style, and consequently they are loyal to the organization embedding TQM. It is argued that because of this reason the total quality management implementation was first successfully implemented in Japan long before it was in the US. Implementing TQM is not as easy as expected. It needs a life-long learning process, a continuous improvement, and a high commitment to quality.

Learning to Live Together Scott et al. (1999) [21] described how TQM needs not only a good system, but also an integrated life-style necessitating the ability to live together. Employee, customer, and supplier involvements are essential to quality and organizational success. Such efforts must include participation by top management in order to have clear aim, redesign of products and process, innovation, and plans and actions that support the organization's strategies. The final and most important stage in Total Quality Management implementation is how to acclimatize a condition where all members live together in harmony to achieve the total quality.

Senge (1993) [22] argues that to excel in an increasingly complex and dynamic world, organizations will have to provide for and encourage individuals and teams in all levels of the organization to learn. He envisions 'learning organizations are places where people continually expand their capacity to create the results they truly desire, where new and expansive patterns of thinking are nurtured, where collective aspiration is set free, and where people are continually learning how to learn together'. In TQM, learning to live together is a crucially important part of the learning process as this management system needs people supporting it.

Total Quality Management consists of many components and methods such as: Deming's 14 principles of Total Quality Management: As the 'father' of TQM, Deming formulated the main beliefs required in implementing TQM (Deming, 1982). [23]

1. Create constancy of purpose toward improvement of product and service with a plan to become competitive and to stay in business. Decide whom top management is responsible to.
2. Adopt the new philosophy. We are in a new economic age. We can no longer live with commonly accepted levels of delays, mistakes, defective materials, and defective workmanship.
3. Cease dependence on mass inspection. Require, instead,

statistical evidence that quality is built in (prevent defects rather than detect defects).

4. End the practice of awarding business on the basis of price tag. Instead, depend on meaningful measures of quality, along with price. Eliminate suppliers that cannot qualify with statistical evidence of quality.
5. Find problems. It is management's job to work continually on the system (design, incoming materials, composition of material, maintenance, improvement of machine, training, supervision, retraining institute modern methods of training on the job).
6. The responsibility of foremen must be changed from sheer numbers to quality [which] will automatically improve productivity.
7. Management must prepare to take immediate action on reports from foremen concerning barriers such as inherited defects, machines not maintained, poor tools, fuzzy operational definitions.
8. Drive out fear, so that everyone may work effectively for the company.
9. Break down barriers between departments. People in research, design, sales, and production must work as a team, to foresee problems of production that may be encountered with various materials and specifications.
10. Eliminate numerical goals, posters, and slogans for the work force, asking for new levels of productivity without providing methods.
11. Eliminate work standards that prescribe numerical quotas.
12. Remove barriers that stand between the hourly worker and his right to pride of workmanship.
13. Institute a vigorous program of education and retraining.
14. Create a structure in top management that will push every day on the above 13 points.

Human needs may well include fundamental or universal aspects, but their importance and the ways in which they learn is different in varied cultures. In the past, there were some resistances by the eastern countries in adopting western practices due to the resentment of colonialism. In a more radical way, Prakash and Esteva (1999) [24] argued fervently that education, particularly at the margins of the industrialized world, as a form of colonialism. Being more advanced in many ways during the late centuries, the western society tend to consider practices from the eastern countries as less sophisticated.

Therefore, it is quite possible that the tardiness in adopting the Japanese style Total Quality Management by American companies was due to this contemplation. It was until the world recognized the advantages and results of outstanding Japanese firms applying TQM, then American companies began to learn and implement this practice.

Deming (1982) [25] points out that many innovations have occurred because the creator of a product or service was able to develop a new idea that was not even imagined by the customer.

The words 'Total Quality' used together are usually meant to recognize that real quality requires all elements of the organization to work together toward achieving that end. It means to strive for excellence in everything an organization does.

Peters and Waterman believe that seven factors are essential for change viz., shared values, strategy, systems, staffing, style, structure and skills (the 7 'S') model..

The three S's–strategy, structure and systems are called as 3 hard Ss while the remaining 4 Ss–staff, skills, styles and shared values are called as 4 soft Ss.

The 4 soft Ss supplement the 3 hard Ss. Organizations which blend the hard Ss with the soft Ss mark TQM a dominant force within their culture. The three hard Ss alone will not be sufficient of establish success in the long run. Since TQM comes from the people, it is not possible to gain the benefits of TQM without the use of 4 soft Ss namely staff, skills, styles and shared values. Creativity, flexibility, teamwork, participation, continuous improvement and leadership are critical to the success of TQM.

Considering the differences in organizations with regard to total quality management, the authors try to elucidate some general characteristics that the work with the described core values of TQM will indicate in the contest of organizations. Due to heterogeneity with thin the small organization area, these characteristics may, however be adequate for some organizations.

Top Management Commitment: Managing human resources can be a source for developing a competitive advantage, since management often is close to the workforce and there is little functional differentiation. The necessary cultural change, implied by TQM, may be more easily realized in organizations if the management espouse the vision and have the leadership skills to enthuse and gain the commitment of their workforce.

Focus on Customers: Focusing on customers would benefit the organizations. Many organizations which are customer focused more are enjoying the market share in the competitive situations. Many organizations depend upon customer relations which makes easy to maintain and improve customer focus and conduct customer research.

Everybody's Commitment: Organizations would have greater potential for success in this area if the management believes in employee involvement and the value of employees as intelligent human beings.

Focus on Process: Organizations have a natural tendency for cross-functional training because they have fewer layers of management and staff. This facilitates the employees to have greater knowledge about the process owners and in what way their work is a part of the resulting product of service.

Continuous Improvement: In the organizations if the employees have a very good sense of the overall profitability of the organization, it would benefit both the employees and the management. They need to be committed and try to improve the business because they know it will directly affect them.

Base Decisions on Facts: To achieve customer satisfaction, decisions must be based on facts, and results must be measured. Fewer layers of management result in easier and less bureaucratic communication and co-ordination between staff, which makes the decision process easier.

The EFQM is a non-prescriptive framework based on nine criteria. Five of these 'Enablers' and four are 'Results'. The 'Enabler' criteria cover what an organization does. The 'Results' criteria cover what an organization achieves. 'Results' are cause by 'Enablers' and feedback from 'Results' help to improve 'Enablers'.

The model, which recognizes there are many approaches to achieving sustainable excellence in all aspects of performance, is based on the premise that excellent results with respect to Performance, Customers, People and Society are achieved through Partnerships and Resources and Processes. The arrows emphasise the dynamic nature of model. They show innovation and learning helping to improve enablers that in turn lead to improved results. The Model's 9 boxes, shown above represent criteria against which to assess an organisation's progress towards excellence. Each of the nine criteria has a definition, which explains the high level meaning of that criterion. To develop the high level meaning further each criterion is supported by a number of sub-criteria pose a number of questions that should be considered in the course of an assessment.

2.8 Role of Quality Circles in Total Quality Management

A quality circle or quality control circle (Q.C. circle) is a small group of employees (average number of nine) who volunteer to meet regularly to undertake work related projects designed to improve working conditions, spur mutual self-development and to advance the company, all by using quality control concepts.

The quality circle was originated in Japan. It is a small work group that meets periodically to discuss ways to improve quality, productivity, or the work environment. In Japan, management or a committee assigns problems to circles. The circle then defines and refines the problem into projects. Analysis, solution, presentation, and implementation follow. Just-in-time (JIT) production: a system of managing operations with little or no delay time or idle inventories between one process and the next with the purpose of efficiency and therefore optimising the quality. JIT inventory control system was originally developed in Japan by Taiichi Okno, a vice president of Toyota (Scott, 1999). [26] Initially the system was called the kanban system, named after the cards that were placed in the parts bins that were used to call for new supply.

The idea behind the system is that the firm should keep a minimum level of inventory on hand, relying on suppliers to furnish parts 'just-in-time' for them to be assembled. This is a direct contrast to the traditional inventory philosophy of US firms, which is sometimes referred to as 'just-in-case' system, which keep healthy levels of safety stocks to ensure that production will not be interrupted. Although large inventory may not a bad idea when interest rates are low, when interest rates are high they become very costly. JIT is not merely a method for reducing inventory. It should be viewed broadly as a procedure for helping companies to manage and reduce their total processing times and therefore improve quality.

The new supplier-customer relationships to ensure total quality: Out of the concept of total quality management (TQM), which is a company-wide system approach to quality, has come a new philosophy of 'love thy supplier' (Scott, 1999). [27] Under this approach, the traditional antagonistic relationship between suppliers and customers, where suppliers are coldly dropped when a cheaper source can be found, is being replaced by a new order in customer-supplier relationship.

In effect, what began as an effort to increase quality

through closer supplier relations has turned to have unexpected benefits. Close customer relationships have helped trim costs, in part, by allowing for the production of higher quality products. This close customer-supplier relationship has allowed the TQM philosophy to be passed across company boundaries to the suppliers, enabling the firm to tap the supplier's expertise in designing higher-quality products.

2.9 Conclusion

TQM encourages participation amongst shop floor workers and managers. There is no single theoretical formalization of total quality, but Deming, Juran and Ishikawa provide the core assumptions, as a "...discipline and philosophy of management which institutionalizes planned and continuous improvement and assumes that quality is the outcome of all activities that take place within an organization; that all functions and all employees have to participate in the improvement process; that organizations need both quality systems and a quality culture".

Total Quality Management (TQM) generally refers to a comprehensive system whereby companies are able to achieve extraordinary levels of quality in their delivered products and services. TQM implementation encloses the four pillars of life-long learning for it is a continuous improvement process that should be done continuously. Despite of the early implementation by the Japanese, based on some researches done by experts, TQM contributes to success more in Japanese firms than in US firms. Accomplishment differences might be due to strategy shaping, frames of reference and cultural background. As a process, the accomplishment of life-long learning in form of TQM depends upon the people executing it. Interactions among people within and outside the organization, how they interrelate, intermingle, cooperate, and link up one to another are factors contributing success to TQM. These senses are not created instantly; people need to learn how to nurture them together. Nurturing TQM characters would be done by living together harmoniously. Living together is a matter of socialism. Socialisation is a process of sharing experiences and creating tacit knowledge such as shared mental models, technical skills, and competence.

The key to acquiring tacit knowledge is experience. Without some form of shared experience, it is extremely difficult for one person to project her or himself into another individual's thinking process. The transfer of information will often make sense, if it is abstracted from associated emotions and specific contexts in which shared experiences are embedded (Nonaka and Takeuchi, 1995). [28] In conclusion, TQM is only a tool to achieve total quality. No tool, TQM included, is effective if exercised improperly. TQM is optimally implemented in an organization which members are committed to a life-long learning process of improving continuously.

The next chapter deals with the management of stress in the organization. The basic concept of stress, root causes of stress, impact of stress on mind and body, role of stressors, stress models, and stress overcoming strategies have been highlighted. Stress has become part of every walks of life. To know the significant role played by the stress this chapter would give a clear understanding to manage the stress in personal and professional life.

Notes

1. Hayes, Treasa (1997) The Learning Organisation: Fashionable Fad or Path to Progress? www.globalresearchbusiness.com.
2. Deming, W. Edwards (1982) Quality Productivity and Competitive Position Cambridge, Mass.: MIT, Centre for Advanced Engineering Study.
3. Barnett, R. (2000) Working Knowledge. In Garrick and Rhodes (2000) Research and Knowledge at Work: Perspective, Case studies and Innovative Strategies, London: Routledge.
4. Ibid.
5. Clarke, T., Rollo, C. (2001) Corporate initiatives in knowledge management. Education + Training, p. 43.
6. Zack, M. (1999) Developing a Knowledge Strategy. California

Management Review. 41, 125-144.
7. Op cit.
8. Op cit.
9. Op cit.
10. Op cit.
11. Petersen, Peter B. (1999) Total Quality Management and The Deming Approach To Quality Management. Journal of Management History 5, 8, 468-488.
12. Kotter, J.P. (1996) Leading Change Boston: Harvard Business School Press.
13. Eraut, M., Alderton, J., Cole, G., Senker, P. (1998) Learning from Other People at Work. In Coffield, F. (ed.), Learning at Work. Bristol: The Policy Press.
14. Argyris, Chris (1994) Good Communication That Blocks Learning Harvard Business Review, 72, 74, 77-85, July-August 1994.
15. Clarke, T., Rollo, C. (2001) Corporate initiatives in knowledge management. Education + Training, 43, 4/5.
16. Compaq (1999) Knowledge Management: Approaching Solutions. White Paper, Compaq Computer Corporation, Houston, TX.
17. Ibid.
18. Argyris, Chris (1991) Teaching Smart People How to Learn Harvard Business Review, 69, 3, 99-109.
19. Lincoln, James R. (1989) Employee Work Attitudes and Management Practice in the US and Japan: Evidence from a Large Comparative Survey. California Management Review, 89-106.
20. Scott, D.F., Martin, J.D., Petty, J.W., and Keown, A.J. (1999) Basic Financial Management. New Jersey: Prentice Hall International Inc.
21. Op cit.
22. Senge, Peter (1993) The Fifth Discipline: The Art and Practice of the Learning Organization.
23. Ibid.
24. Prakash, M.S., Esteva, G. (1998) Escaping Education: Living as Learning within Grassroots Cultures. New York: Peter Lang.
25. Ibid.
26. Scott, D.F., Martin, J.D., Petty, J.W., and Keown, A.J. (1999) Basic Financial Management. New Jersey: Prentice Hall

International Inc.

27. Ibid.
28. Nonaka, I., Takeuchi, H. (1995) The Knowledge-Creating Company: How Japanese Companies Create the Dynamics of Innovation. New York: Oxford University Press.

3

TQM for Managing Stress

3.1 Introduction

Creating a high performance organization is a focal point in the training and development. Creating a high performance organization requires understanding what factors influence performance. The factors include economic environment, increased competition, more demanding customer expectations, work culture, work relations, work climate, personality factors of employees, traits, and stress causing elements. One of the most significant factors is stress. Historically, stress has been viewed as an inevitable consequence of work life; or at most, a health care issue. Stress interferes with human intellectual, emotional and inter-personal functioning. In fact, nearly every popular training and organizational development initiative is directly compromised of the intellectual, emotional and interpersonal consequences of stress.

Stress is part of everyday life for human factor. Stress refers to the demands, pressures or forces applied to human resources in an organisation. Stress also involves perception of threat about internal or external events. Threat stimulates the release of stress hormones which produce the 'fight-flight' response. The fight-flight response leads to physical, emotional and mental action which is essential for survival of employees in an organization. Initiatives like The Learning Organisation, Process Re-engineering, Diversity Training, Collaborative Team Work, and The High Performance Organisations are all affected by the way people perceive and respond to stress. The nature and environment of work is changing at greater pace. Perhaps now more than ever before, job stress posses a critical threat to the health of workers and in turn, to the health of organization.

When employees face the stressors a psychological imbalance takes place as a result of which fight-flight hormones are still activated. As an employee does not respond physically to these stressors, the hormones remain in human bodies leading to ongoing feelings of tension and anxiety. Positive management of stress results in positive emotions such as enjoyment, satisfaction, enthusiasm and excitement. However, too much stress can be debilitating when it causes detrimental changes in how one thinks, feels and behaves. Stress has been a much and widely talked about phenomenon in the industrial world. It has featured in the Indian industrial organisations since 80's when the Indian market turned competitive. By now stress has become a major buzzword and legitimate concern of the times because it causes harm to both employees and organisations. To quote, a recent estimate is that stress is costing corporate America a staggering US$ 68 billion annually in lost productivity due to absences from work and stress claims costing up to 10 percent of company's earnings. It further reports that up to 90 percent of patients complain of stress-related symptoms and disorders. [1] What is true of corporate America is true of corporate India also. [2] Corporate employees stress has become a crucial factor in the recent past.

Work-related stress is a pattern of physiological, emotional, cognitive and behavioural reactions to some extremely taxing aspects of work content, work organization and work environment. When people experience work-related stress, they often feel tense and distressed and feel they cannot cope. Due to globalisation and changes in the nature of work, people in developing countries have to deal with increasing work-related stress. In industrialized countries people are becoming more familiar with what work-related stress is and how to manage it (e.g. WHO, 2003; [3] WHO, 2003), [4] however, in developing countries, this may not yet be the case. Although a few studies have been conducted in developing countries, particularly in Latin America, there are still not enough in-depth studies to fully analyse both cultural differences and behaviours which vary from one country to another. Along with existing difficulties in controlling other more well-known occupational risks, there is a lack of awareness of work-related stress, and shortage of resources to deal with it.

Cultural aspects may need some attention when dealing with work-related stress in developing countries. For example, spirituality and religion, next to community rituals are often more important than acquisition of material possessions or money. For women workers, social resources for taking care of their families are usually available in the formal economic sector. However, resources for the daily life logistics are not updated with the technology applied to community and private services in most of the developed countries, such as payment of bills by mail, phone or internet. Even when this type of service exists in some countries, the majority of workers do not have access to them.

Therefore, daily routine tasks can be time-consuming and daunting. The level of development in most of the developing countries implies drastic differences between urban and rural areas in the availability of resources, income and jobs. Globalization and commercial agreements with developed countries and the World Bank rules have resulted in a decrease in investment in agricultural activities. As a consequence, along with the population growth, the offer of labour in urban and suburban areas, where industry and services settled, increased enormously. On the other hand, deregulation has also been the requirement during the globalization process, which has been translated into less protection of worker's rights, particularly health and retirement benefits, as well as less job security. As a result there is increased unemployment and under-employment and people are forced to accept substandard jobs. Further, it is often the case that power in institutions and companies is unequally distributed.

For individuals in developing countries, context often plays an important role in determining their perception, attribution and behaviour and it is often believed that the cause and control of outcomes is determined by external circumstances. Such cultural aspects influence what people perceive as good working conditions. When the only choice is to accept authority or to lose one's job, workers often accept substandard working conditions, because they know it is an employers market.

In developing countries the largest part of the workforce is self-employed, occupied in small companies and household industries. They belong to the 'informal sector' of the economy. These companies or individuals often lack the resources and infrastructure to protect their workers or themselves from work-related stress and their groups of workers are difficult to reach both in terms of information dissemination and assistance. In addition, the lack of policy development in relation to psychosocial risks and work related stress makes it difficult for companies of all sizes to put into place effective control strategies to deal with these issues. The situation is made worse by the lack of occupational health services coverage. WHO estimates that worldwide only 5-10 percent of the workers in developing countries and 20-50 percent of the workers in industrialized countries (with a few exceptions) have access to adequate occupational health services (WHO, 2003). [5] Work-related psychosocial issues are rarely dealt by these even where they are available.

Work-related stress in developing countries is often made worse by a broad spectrum of factors outside the work environment from gender inequalities, poor paths of participation and poor environmental management of industrial pollution to illiteracy, parasitic and infectious diseases, poor hygiene and sanitation, poor nutrition, poor living conditions, inadequate transportation systems and general poverty. Overwhelming problems linked to globalization are unemployment, under and self-employment, precariousness of working conditions due to new systems of work organization and liberalization of the industrial relations. Globalization has led to growing inequality and decreasing prioritisation of social aspects in many parts of the world.

3.2 Work and Health in Developing and Developed Countries

1. About 75 percent of the world's labour force (which counts about 2400 million people) lives and works in developing countries.
2. 20-50 percent of workers in industrialized countries may be subjected to hazardous exposures at work and this rate is expected to be higher in the developing and newly industrialized countries.
3. 50 percent of workers in industrialized countries judge their work to be "mentally demanding".
4. Each year there are about 120 million occupational accident injuries with 200,000 occupational fatalities and 68-157 million cases of occupational disease among the global work force.
5. More than 80 percent of the workforce consists of small and medium-sized enterprises. In developing countries it is estimated to be even more and the largest workforce is to be found in the informal sector. Small and medium-sized enterprises, in particular, as well as the informal sector have poor access to occupational health and safety services and other external support. They often lack knowledge about occupational health in general.
6. Poor occupational health and reduced working capacity of workers may cause economic loss up to 10-20 percent of the Gross National Product of a country. Globally occupational deaths, diseases, and illnesses account for an estimated loss of 4 percent of the gross domestic product. [6]

The year 1991 is stated as a remarkable year and mile stone in the history of Indian economy as India focused on new economic policies like globalization, liberalization and privatization. This new approach has strengthened India's economic status with the entry of multinational corporations. India has emerged as challenging nation in the world due to its tremendous changes in socio economic policies.

3.3 Statistical Evidence on Stress in India

In order to meet the demands of international markets, the Indian organizations are focusing on performance which is linked with stress. The May 19, 2007 report of survey conducted by India's industry body Assocham has revealed that " the menace of stress and mental fatigue has intensified in recent times at the top and middle positions of sectors comprising construction, shipping, banks, government hospitals, trading houses, electronic and print media, small-scale industries, retail and card franchise companies." Working conditions also emerged as an important factor which contributes to the stress level of employees. The survey of nearly 200 Indian employees revealed that top executives such as civil engineers, marketing managers, quality controllers, editors, reporters and copy writers brave stress and take home its adverse impact.

Another survey conducted by BC Corporate Bureau in New Delhi reported on July 10, 2006 stated that out of 270 CMDs percent said that stress level was moderate for them, while 11 percent was too much. About 70 percent of industry leaders coping with work pressure suffered more from mental stress than physical strain. According to the report of Grant Thornton International Business Owners Survey 2006, India's high turnover growth is linked to high stress. With regard to job security concerns highest in dynamic economies India, Japan and Thailand proportion approached to almost 50 percent which indicates contribution of concern about job security to stress level is almost 50 percent. This shows in general worries about job security are greatest in dynamic, strongly expanding economies.

In modern organisations stress plays a critical role in focussing on total quality management. Organisations' survival is depends on the role of total quality management which is linked with stress. Stress is defined as a non-specific response of the body to a stimulus or event (stressor). Under a general model of the stress response, when an individual experiences a stressor, the stressor will lead to a physiological response, one that can be measured by several indicators, such as elevated heart rate. In related literature, the term "stress" is used to refer to this physiological response. Stressors vary in form and can include extreme temperature or lighting, time pressure, lack of sleep, and exposure to threat or danger, among others. All stressors, however, tend to produce similar physiological responses within the body (Selye, 1956). [7] Stressors involved in peacekeeping and combat operations overlap, but they are also somewhat distinct. Some of the most significant stressors associated with both types of deployments are uncertainty, long work hours, risk of death or disease, boredom, and separation from family (Halverson, 1995 [8] and Campbell 1998). [9]

There is a need for the organisations to focus on maintaining stress in relevant otherwise it would harm the organisation functioning. Stress causes to improve the performance when it is maintained in a particular way and when the stress level increases it causes decline in performance and it would have impact on organisation's total quality management. Stress is inevitable in human life. There is, therefore, no way out but to fight with stress or cope with it. The coping with stress will obviously relate to dealing with the already occurred stressors and avoiding the occurrence of potential stress. One way to cope with and avoid stress may be making the people aware of undesirable consequences of stress through mass media, followed by coping strategies required to be adopted. This make the people realize about the harmful effects of stress. Such realisation will in turn prepare the people to adopt the self-help or self-control strategies, which have proved effective to tackle stress.

Over the past three decades, there has been a growing belief in all sectors of employment and in government that the experience of stress at work has undesirable consequences for the health and safety of individuals and for the health of the organisation. This belief has been reflected both in public and media interest and in increasing concern voiced by the trade unions, and professional and scientific bodies. There are three basic questions that need to be answered in regard to stress:

- What is the nature of stress at work and the root causes of it?
- Does work stress affect health and well-being of employees and, if so, how?
- What are the implications of existing research for the management of work related stress in the organisation?

There are several contradictory assumptions about how stressors in organizations affect performance and total quality management. The TQM can be possible when performance is given top priority in the organizations. It is plausible to assume that stressors have a negative linear effect on performance. Such a negative effect can be explained by direct and indirect effects. The direct effect implies that stressors, particularly situational constraints make task accomplishment more difficult, if not impossible. For example, in case a task has to be accomplished with specific technical equipment and this equipment is not available because of a computer breakdown, task performance will suffer directly.

Moreover, stressors may indirectly affect performance by decreasing alertness or motivation which in turn negatively affects performance. There is a long tradition in conducting laboratory studies on the task performance-effects of stressors (Postman and Bruner, 1948). [10] These studies show that the exposure to stressors leads to cognitive reactions such as Stress in Organizations narrowed attention including a focus on salient cues and reduced working memory capacity. A reduced working memory capacity is associated with a speed/accuracy trade off when working under stressful conditions, particularly under time pressure. Moreover, narrowed attention and reduced working memory capacity have an impact on decision making strategies.

More specifically, they result in simpler decision strategies, recognition rather those analytical strategies, and less complete mental simulations (Klein, 1996). [11] Recent studies suggest that the effects of stressors on performance are mediated by fatigue (Hockey, Maule, Vlough, and Bdzola, 2000 [12]). Some of these effects of stressors were also found in more realistic simulations of work environments. For example, simulated workload resulted in a performance decrease in some studies although not in all (Shaw and Weekley, 1985). [13] When using a mail sorting task, Searle (1999) [14] found that high job demands (i.e., high work load) were associated with an increase in performance attempts, but also with a reduction in performance accuracy, particularly in situations with low control.

In contrast to these findings from laboratory and simulation studies, findings from field studies are far less consistent. With respect to task performance, some stressors were found to be related to impaired performance, while others were not. For example, in a study on secretaries' job performance Spector, Dwyer, and Jex (1988) [15] reported a negative relationship between secretaries' perceptions of constraints and ambiguity with supervisory performance ratings. But no significant relationships between secretaries' perceptions of workload or conflict and supervisory performance ratings emerged. Similarly, Beehr, Jex, Stacy, and Murray (2000) [16] found negative relationships between specific stressors (i.e., acute stressful events, chronic occupation specific stressors and workload variability) and an objective financial performance measure of door-to-door book sellers, but a positive relationship between role overload and job performance. In a classic study of engineers and scientists, Andrews and Farris (1972) [17] reported that experienced time pressure increased subsequent performance.

One of the best studies (Jones 1988) [18] showed that stressors at work increase the likelihood of errors and that an organization wide stress management program and changes in management of the hospitals reduced malpractice. All these results point to the need to develop a more specific theory of how stressors are related to performance. Evidence from meta-analyses suggests that there is no substantial relationship between role stressors such as role ambiguity or role conflict and job performance, at least when job performance is assessed by objective measures or supervisory/peer ratings (Jackson and Schuler, 1985; [19] Tubbs and Collins, 2000). [20] Findings Stress in Organizations from field studies on the performance effects of situational constraints is inconclusive as well. Some studies found performance deteriorating effects of situational constraints, while others did not (Jex, 1998). [21] There are several explanations for the lack of substantial linear relationships between stressors and job performance in field studies.

First, one might assume a curvilinear relationship between stressors and performance. This would imply that the performance effects of stressors are not uniform across all degrees of stressor intensity. The relationship between arousal and performance, performance might increase as stressors increase up to a moderate degree; when stressors become too high, however, performance might decrease. Studies which tested the assumed curvilinear relationship between stressors and performance failed to find such a relationship (Westman and Eden, 1996). [22]

Second, the relationship between stressors and job performance might be moderated by other variables. Such moderator variables might include individual competence (Payne 1991) [23] or work commitment (Jamal, 1985). [24] However until now, empirical evidence for the existence of such moderator effects is weak (Jex, 1998). [25]

Third, the performance measures used in most of the field

studies might be too global for showing a performance deteriorization effect of work stressors. For example, a study by Kjellberg, Sköldström, Anderson, and Lindberg (1996) [26] suggests that specific performance measures such as reaction times show decrements under stress in a field setting.

Fourth, possibly there is essentially no–or no large-effect of stressors on performance in field settings. This interpretation would contradict findings from laboratory studies that showed stressors to impair basic cognitive processes. However, impairment of basic cognitive processes may not necessarily translate into a decrease in overall job performance in real-life work settings. Individuals are able to compensate for the effects of stressors, for example by switching to different task strategies (Sperandio, 1971). [27]

Hockey (2000) [28] offers an additional explanation for the inconsistency between laboratory and field study results: Many laboratory tasks are relatively simple, trivial and under-learned. If stressors occur in such a situation, study participants have little possibilities to switch to different strategies, be it because of a lack of skills in the specific task, or because of the restrictions of the laboratory setting. Real-life work tasks however, are usually well-learned and complex. If stressors occur in these real-life situations, individuals often possess the necessary skills to pursue different strategies.

Moreover, in organizational settings, goal attainment has high priority. This implies that task performance must be protected, if necessary, at the expense of increased effort or neglect of subsidiary activities. Klein (1996) [29] additionally argues that some of the cognitive strategies affected by stressors in laboratory settings play a minor role in real-life settings. For example, analytical decision strategies suffer from time pressure, but Stress in Organizations such strategies are rarely used in naturally decision making; therefore, the negative impact of performance is limited.

There are a few studies which examined the relationship between stressors and contextual performance. For example,

Motowidlo, Packard, and Manning (1986) [30] reported negative relationships between the intensity and frequency of stressful events on the one hand and interpersonal aspects of job performance of nurses on the other hand. Jex (1998) [31] tested whether situational constraints were related to organizational citizenship behaviour (OCB) and reported negative relationships between situational constraints and three aspects of OCB. These findings suggest that in stress situations individuals assign priority to maintain task performance, at the expense of discretionary behaviours such as contextual performance. However, a longitudinal study by Fay and Sonnentag (2001) [32] suggests that the experience of stressors at work can even have an enhancing effect on one extra-role performance-personal initiative. Similarly, Bunce and West (1994) [33] reported that health care professionals responded with innovations to the experience of stressors at work. Taken together, laboratory studies showed that stressors impair basic cognitive processes.

However, as field studies indicate, this impairment does not necessarily result in a decrease in overall job performance. Particularly workload was found to be associated with higher job performance. These findings suggest that individuals spend more effort, prioritize the most relevant tasks and use compensatory strategies for upholding their performance under stressful situations. It remains unclear if and how such a 'performance management' strategy is associated with health or well-being effects. It might be that such an approach exhausts an individual's resources in the long run and, therefore, affects an individual's health and well-being in a negative way.

Total Quality Management (TQM) programmes had their introduction to U.S. companies in the 1980s in response to the competitive onslaught of Japanese companies in the automobile and electronics industries. Companies in many other industries quickly followed, as did a consulting industry to help companies adopt TQM. TQM is viewed as the continuous improvement of work processes to enhance the organization's ability to deliver high quality products or services in a cost-effective manner (Spector and Beer, 1994). [34] It typically involves a number of interventions. These are explicit identification of customer requirements, cross functional teams, selection of suppliers based on quality, the use of a variety of technical (scientific) methods to enhance analysis and process management methods for enhancing team effectiveness (Hackman and Wageman, 1995). [35] TQM also involves a multiple stakeholder philosophy that values equally community, customers and employees. Implicit in this philosophy are values of teamwork and collaboration.

There is little question that when implemented properly, TQM can have a dramatic impact on the performance and culture of an organization (Deming, 1986 [36]; Juran 1989 [37]; Buzzell and Gale, 1987 [38]; Hackman and Wegeman, 1995 [39]; Lawler, 1998). [40] In recent studies confirm these assessments. By comparing the performance of firms who have received quality awards with a matched control group of firms who have not, Hendricks and Singhal (1997) [41] have shown that firms receiving quality awards outperform the control group in operating income and revenues over a ten year period. In a second study Hendricks and Singhal (2001) [42] show that the long run stock performance 3 of firms who receive quality awards is far higher (38 percent to 46 percent) than a matched control group of companies who did not receive such an award. These stock performance improvements are found in the five-year post implementation period, not in the first five year implementation period.

The fact that improvement in the stock performance only occurred after five years of implementation, suggests that a TQM transformation is a long-term process requiring a fundamental shift in management practice and culture. This may explain why there have also been a plethora of studies questioning the value of TQM, many by consulting firms who work with their clients to implement TQM (see, for example, the International Quality Study, a joint study by Ernst and Young and the American Quality Foundation (1992) [43] and Kelly (1992) [44] who presents studies done by Arthur D. Little Inc. and Rath and Strong).

According to these studies, senior management in some 60 to 70 percent of firms feel that quality improvement efforts have not boosted their capacity to compete, have not resulted in implementation of a significant number of practices associated with TQM and have not focused TQM improvement on improved products and services. In this thesis I postulate that failures of TQM implementation not TQM theory and method. Failures occur because senior management tends to motivate change through top-down programs (Beer, 1990; [45] Schaffer, 1998) [46]. Failure to solicit and receive feedback about potential gaps between their TQM rhetoric and the reality of implementation (Zbaracki, 1998) [47] prevents senior management from learning how their own actions and policies may be responsible for the gap and then making changes accordingly. Top down programs also undermine unit leaders commitment and their capacity to lead a TQM transformation in their unit.

A primary role of management is to lead an organization in its day-to-day operations as well as to maintain it as a viable entity into the future. Quality has become an important factor to success in this latter strategic responsibility. An organization's goals can be achieved when people put in their best effort. Employee assessment is one of the fundamental jobs of HRM, but not as easily as though, unless one knows the strengths and weakness of employee and specify the area of programs no matter how scientifically planned, would be aimed at correct lines. An effective appraisal system reduces the change happening and introduces rationality into management. It also provides the management a tool to review the career of its manager and match their aspirations with job opportunities.

Quality has been a tradition in India and monuments,

relics, handicrafts, gems, jewellery and craftsmanship has woven quality into our heritage. But while quality was a way of managing business in the US and Japan in the 1950s, it was not so in India. The Quality movement was consolidated in the 1980s in the Indian industries to bring about a synergy of resources by the pioneering efforts of Confederation of Indian Industries. Performance which is focussed towards Total Quality Management is management approaches that originated in the 1950's and has steadily become more popular since the early 1980's. Total Quality is a description of the culture, attitude and organization of a company that strives to provide customers with products and services that satisfy their needs. The culture requires quality in all aspects of the company's operations, with processes being done right the first time and defects and waste eradicated from operations. [48]

Total Quality Management, TQM, is a method by which management and employees can become involved in the continuous improvement of the production of goods and services. It is a combination of quality and management tools aimed at increasing business and reducing losses due to wasteful practices. A few leading companies which have implemented TQM include Ford Motor Company, Phillips Semiconductor, SGL Carbon, Motorola and Toyota Motor Company. In the late 1980s, providing customer satisfaction in customer terms became a specific goal of business organisation. Providing high quality was recognized as a key element for success. At the end of the twentieth century, business organizations were involved in what has become a quality revolution. It began in Japan and has spread to other parts of the world. It involves an entirely new way of thinking about and dealing with quality that encompasses the entire organisation. Different nomenclature has been used to denote this "six sigma" at Motorola, "Leadership through quality" at Xerox, "perfect Design Quality" at Intel and "Total Quality Control" at Hewlett-Packard, but more often referred to as "Total Quality Management".

3.4 Select Review of Literature

There are numerous reviews of research into psychosocial hazards and stress and a large number of studies dealing with the stressors in almost every conceivable work setting and occupation. However, research into the nature and effects of a hazard is not the same as assessment of the associated risk. Indeed, most published studies would provide very little data that could be used for a risk assessment. Many "stress surveys" tend to identify only hazards or only outcomes, whereas the object of a risk assessment is to establish an association between hazards and health outcomes, and to evaluate the risk to health from exposure to a hazard.

An almost unavoidable corollary of the paucity of adequate risk assessments is that most "stress management" interventions target the individual rather than the organisation (the former is usually seen as cheaper and less cumbersome), are often off-the-shelf designs, and are entirely divorced from the process of diagnosis of the problems if diagnosis takes place at all.

A different type of approach is therefore required in order to carry out risk assessments which can then inform the design of interventions in other words, a strategy that actually asks the question before giving the answer. Such a strategy has already been suggested for the management of physical hazards at work place which has been defined as "the systematic process by which hazards are identified, risks analysed and managed, and workers protected". As a systematic and comprehensive approach to assessing the risks within the work environment, the control cycle satisfies current legal requirements. However, it is still necessary to evaluate whether it represents a scientifically valid and reliable strategy to assess psychosocial hazards.

The term stress is used to connote a variety of meanings both by the common man and psychologists. Psychologists of different persuasions have given (a) stimulus-oriented, (b) response-oriented (both physiological and behavioural) definitions of the term, and depth psychologists have treated the concept from the etiological and psycho-dynamic viewpoints. It appears that under these circumstances the essential features of the stress experience have not received the attention they deserve (Asthana, 1983) [49].

Stress at work resulting from increased complexity of work and its divergent demands have become prominent features of the modern organisation giving rise to impairing effects on employees physical as well as psychological well being. Though a moderate degree of stress has been noted as creating as well as promoting employee's inclination towards the job, excessive and consistent job stress results in job dissatisfaction, tension, anxiety, depression and in some cases even serious mental and physical disabilities ranging all the way to coronary diseases (Srivasthava, 1991) [50]. Research findings suggest that when an individual comes under stress, his cognitive performance and decision making may be adversely affected. Notably, under conditions of stress, individuals are likely to screen out peripheral stimuli (Easterbrook, 1959 [51]; Janis and Mann, 1977) [52] make decisions based on heuristics (rules of thumb or guidelines) (Shaham, Singer, and Schaeffer, 1992 [53]; Klein,1996) [54] suffer from performance rigidity or narrow thinking (Friedman and Mann, 1993 [55]; Keinan, 1987) [56] lose their ability to analyse complicated situations and manipulate information (Larsen, 2001) [57] task completion time may be increased and accuracy reduced by stress (Idzikowski and Baddeley, 1983 [58]; McLeod, 1977) [59].

In addition to effects on the individual, stress has also been shown to negatively affect group functioning. When stressed, individuals are likely to yield control to their superiors and to allow authority to become more concentrated in the upper levels of the hierarchy. Communication effectiveness may also be reduced (Driskell, Carson, and Moskal, 1988) [60]. Stress can also lead to "group think," in which members of the group ignore important cues, force all members to adhere to a consensus decision even an incorrect one and rationalise poor decisions (Janis and Mann, 1977) [61]. Even if some level of stress may have a positive effect on performance as suggested by the U-hypothesis, extended exposure to stress or a single exposure to an extreme stressor can have severe negative consequences on non-task performance dimensions. For example, high levels of stress can lead to emotional exhaustion, lower organizational commitment, and increased turnover intentions (Cropanzano, Rapp, and Bryne, 2003) [62]. In extreme cases, stress can lead to post-traumatic stress disorder (PTSD), a psychiatric illness that can interfere with life functioning. PTSD has a variety of symptoms, including flashbacks, difficulty sleeping, and social isolation.

There is evidence to suggest that work is only one of a number of possible areas or aspects of life that can give rise to the experience of stress and ill-health (Goldberg and Novack, 1992 [63]; Surtees and Wainwright, 1998) [64] largely following on from the work of Selye (1956) [65], there has been an assumption that discrete, time limited 'life events' requiring change or adaptation are associated with the experience of stress and may contribute to a wide range of disorders. Many attempts have been made to identify and scale such stressful life events (Holmes and Rahe, 1967 [66]; Dohrenwend and Dohrenwend, 1974 [67]; Dohrenwend et al., 1988 [68]; Fisher, 1996) [69] while psychometric research into the nature and impact of stressful life events is not without methodological problems (Perkins, 1988) [70] some progress has been made in determining the relative importance of different types of events.

However, it should be noted that where life event scales have included work events, the designers have been concerned only with discrete, 'acute' work-related events, stress causes, consequences and impact of stress on total quality management is mentioned in the later sections of the thesis, it is now widely thought that the primary stressors facing most employees in the course of their working life are chronic rather than acute and are rarely mentioned in life event scales. Some studies have also suggested that rankings of life events are context-dependent and can vary between different countries (Rahe, 1969) [71] and between urban and rural communities (Abel, 1987) [72]. Thus, although at first sight life event scales may seem to answer the question 'how important are work stressors?', in fact, they do not. It is likely that there are interactions between stressors, both acute and chronic, which do not respect the boundary between work and non-work domains.

A review of work motivation by Tiglao (1990) [73] found that both intrinsic and extrinsic motives served as important motivating factors. Orpen (1994) [74] in his study found that personal control moderated the effects of work motivation on job satisfaction and performance, and highly motivated subjects were more adversely affected by low personal control. Furnham, Forde and Ferari (1999) [75] found in their studies that extroverts stressed the importance of motivational factors to them, while neurotics rated hygiene factors as more important to them in choosing a particular job.

Knoop (1994a) [76] tested two predictions from the two-factor theory i.e., the intrinsic work values would have an inverse relationship with stress (individuals with a strong sense of achievement, recognition, responsibility should experience less stress) and that the presence of extrinsic work values would not lead to stress reduction. Knoop (1994b) [77] found that stress correlated negatively with most of the intrinsic work values, but was not consistently related to extrinsic ones.

An underlying often-unstated requirement for TQM interventions to take root is a fundamental transformation of the organization's culture (Schein, 1992 [78]). Organization must unhook themselves from their functional moorings by delegating authority to lower level cross-functional teams who need decision rights to implement process changes using the technical methods of TQM (Hackman and Wegeman, 1995 [79]; Spector and Beer 1994) [80]. In almost all cases this means functional managers will lose power and process team leaders and members gain power. For these change to occur, the basis of power must shift from authority based on position to authority based on knowledge and proximity to problems and information.

For long-term success the organization may also have to consider how financial gains from improvements are going to be allocated so that employee commitment can be sustained (Hackman and Wegeman, 1995 [81]). Finally, management's behaviour and the organization's emergent culture must become consistent over time with the TQM philosophy or employees will become cynical. Such cynicism in turn undermines commitment. Thus, a company seeking to make a fundamental TQM transformation faces significant organizational and managerial change challenges. It is highly likely the difficulty in TQM implementation reported by consultants reflects the programmatic nature of their interventions. Consultants recommend the adoption of cross-functional teams and extensive training in TQM philosophy and methods, for example, but unless senior teams at every level of the company are committed to the ideas they will not realign their own behaviour and the organization's policies and practices to support this new direction. Without that support managers experience a gap between rhetoric and reality, become cynical and under invest their time and energy in managing the transformation in their unit.

As top managers come to realize that top-down programs are not working, they reduce their commitment and withdraw resources (their time and money). As a result TQM becomes a passing fad until the next program is introduced. The proposition that TQM is often seen as a fad and not adopted with deep commitment needed for successful implementation is supported by research. Miller and Hartwick (2002 [82]) found that TQM citations in the business literature began a continuous long-term decline in 1992 after a decade of dramatic increases.

During the same period there was also a marked decline in TQM consulting firms. Further, supporting the conclusion that many TQM initiatives like other best practices are fads, Miller and Hartwick found that the decline in TQM citation was followed by a rise and subsequent decline in business process reengineering (BPE) citations. Commitment to TQM appears to have been only skin deep. These findings are also supported by research about organizational change which finds that top down programs, including TQM, do not lead to fundamental and persistent corporate transformations (Beer, 1990 [83]; Schaffer, 1988) [84].

The superficiality that characterizes too many top-down programs is captured by the following observation of a manager whose company had launched a quality program: "The first quality circle program was very political; everybody noticed who participated and who didn't. Any problems we had in implementing it had to be swept under the rug. All management wanted to know was how many teams had been formed and how much money they had saved." (Beer, 1990) [85] The result in this company was cynicism by employees who saw inconsistencies between management's espoused new TQM direction and the reality of superficial change. "This too will pass," was one of the most frequent responses to new programs, an indication of low commitment, an essential ingredient for fundamental change. Indeed, ten years later the company from which the above quote came, was no longer in existence, a casualty of competition. Spurred by GE's reported success with Six Sigma under Jack Welch, a high status CEO, we are now seeing a resurgence of total quality management initiatives in many companies under this new label.

There is no reason to believe, however, that the implementation of Six Sigma programs in many companies will be any more successful than the programs in earlier years. Innovations like TQM are typically motivated by top management's desire to improve performance. However, if top management adopts TQM because other firms have, understanding of TQM and how it can be utilized to improve performance of the firm will be low. If understanding is low, commitment will also be low and will lead to early abandonment. There is considerable evidence that many firms adopt innovations in management in the hope of rapid painless change as well as legitimacy in the eyes of investors and the business community (DiMaggio and Powell, 1983 [86]; Staw and Epstein, 2000 [87]; Westphal, 1997) [88]. From a change perspective, the adoption of TQM because another high status for companies. CEOs who do so are not likely to be responding to problems defined by a rigorous analysis of barriers to higher performance in their own company. As a result they are unlikely to be launching change with real conviction. This causes these CEOs to delegate the TQM change to a staff group, increasing cynicism as rhetoric and reality diverge over time. In these companies TQM is measured by the number of quality teams and people involved in them, as the quote above suggests, as opposed to an honest assessment of how widely and effectively the company and its local unit leaders' are making TQM an integral part of their organizational unit's practice and culture.

Delegating change to a staff group who launches a program on behalf of the CEO leads to compliance by line managers they respond to the political pressures described in the quote above as opposed to being internally committed. It is not surprising, therefore, that TQM initiatives managed in this manner fail to be sustained. Once a TQM program is launched, it highly unlikely that management will hear the honest truth about gaps between their rhetoric and the actual reality of implementation. Extensive research shows the tendency of lower levels to hide painful truths from senior management (Argyris, 1990 [89]; Beer and Eisenstat, 2000 [90]; Morrison and Milliken, 2000 [91], Zbaracki (1998) [92] found that the reality of TQM implementation in five firms he studied diverged significantly from the rhetoric of top management. Money was being spent on various programs but managers and workers often felt that it was wasted. In these companies, TQM successes are more likely to be reported to top management than difficulties in implementation or complete failures (Mallinger, 1993) [93].

It must be concluded that "the jury is still out" on stress management training: whilst it seems logical that such interventions should promote employee health. The evidence for employee assistance programmes, particularly those broadly conceived to include health promotion in the workplace, may be more encouraging, although it relates to counselling, the provision of counselling is largely designed to assist employees who are already suffering a problem, and is, in that sense, post hoc. Stressor reduction or hazard control is, for several reasons, the most promising area for interventions, although again, there is not yet sufficient information to be confident about the nature and extent of their effectiveness. To date, such conclusions are based more on moral and strategic reasoning than on empirical data, although the data that do exist are supportive. What can be firmly concluded, however, is that there is still a need for further and more adequate evaluation studies.

Unfortunately, there are very few well designed and evaluated such interventions available in the literature to date. Nonetheless, Murphy (1992) [94] conclude that "job redesign and organisational change remain the preferred approaches to stress management because they focus on reducing or eliminating the sources of the problem in the work environment". However, they also point out that such approaches require a detailed audit of work stressors and a knowledge of the dynamics of organisational change if unwelcome outcomes are to be minimised. Further, such interventions can be expensive and more difficult and disruptive to design, implement and evaluate factors which may make them less popular alternatives to secondary (reaction) and tertiary (treatment) interventions.

Nonetheless, Landy (1992) [95] has summarised a number

of possible interventions focused on the design of the work environment, and Murphy (1988) [96] noted that, given the varieties of work stressors that have been identified, many other types of action relating to organisational and work development should be effective in reducing work stress. Van der Hek and Plomp (1997) [97] also concluded that "there is some evidence that organization-wide approaches show the best results on individual, individual-organizational interface and organizational parameters [outcome measures]; these comprehensive programmes have a strong impact on the entire organization, and require the full support of management".

The emerging evidence is strong enough for the United States' National Institute for Occupational Safety and Health (NIOSH) to have identified "the organization of work" as one of the national occupational safety and health priority areas (Rosenstock, 1997) [98]. As part of their National Occupational Research Agenda (NORA), NIOSH intend to focus research on issues such as the impact of work organisation on overall health, the identification of healthy organisation characteristics and the development of intervention strategies. The evaluation literature is inconclusive as to what are the exact mechanisms by which interventions, and particularly those focused on the individual, might affect health. Often, where different types of individually focused interventions have been compared, there is no evidence that any one or any combination is better than any other. This indicates that there may be a general, non-specific effect of intervening: the fact of an intervention may be beneficial, rather than its exact content. Interviews with managers responsible for introducing such interventions suggest that they are aware of such effects (Cox, 1988 [99]).

It is, therefore, possible that at least part of the effects of stress management programmes is due to the way they alter workers' perceptions of, and attitudes to, their organisations, and hence organisational culture. It was argued earlier that poor organisational culture might be associated with an increased experience of stress, while a good organisational culture might weaken or "buffer" the effects of stress on health. A defining factor for organisational culture is the size of the enterprise, and this should be borne in mind when considering intervention and evaluation issues, together with the wider context in terms of the socio-economic environment and work culture of the organisation.

Notes

1. Virginia M. Gibson: Stress in Work Place: A Hidden Cost Factor, H.R. Focus, January, 1993, p. 15.
2. Raju Arisetti: Stress Strikes Corporate World, *Economic Times Esquire*, October, 28, 1989, p. 1.
3. World Health Organization (2003). Authored by: Cassitto, M.G., Fattorini, E., Gilioni, R., Rengo, C. and Gonik, V. 'Raising Awareness of Psychological Harassment at Work'. Geneva: WHO, 2003 (Protecting Workers' Health Series No. 4). Geneva: WHO.
4. World Health Organization (2004). Authored by: Leka, S., Griffiths, A. and Cox, T. Work Organization and Stress: Systematic problem approaches for employers, managers and trade unions representatives. Geneva: WHO (Protecting Workers' Health Series 3). Geneva: World Health Organization (WHO).
5. Op cit, p. 2.
6. http://www.who.int/occupational_health/en/oehstrategy.pdf.
7. Selye, H. The Stress of Life, New York: McGraw-Hill, 1956.
8. Halverson, CPT R., CPT P. Bliese, SGT R. Moore, and CPT C. Castro, *Psychological Well-Being and Physical Health Symptoms Deployed for Operation Uphold Democracy*: A Summary of Human Dimensions Research in Haiti, Washington, D.C.: Walter Reed Army Institute for Research, 1995.
9. Campbell, MAJ S., CPT D. Ritzer, SGT J. Valentine, and COL R. Gifford, *Operation Joint Guard*, Bosnia: *An Assessment of Operational Stress and Adaptive Coping Mechanisms of Soldiers,* Washington, D.C.: Walter Reed Institute of Research, 1998.
10. Postman, L., and Bruner, J. S. (1948). Perception under stress. Psychological Review, 55, 314-323.

11. Klein, G. (1996). The effect of acute stressors on decision making. In J. E. Driskell and E. Salas (Eds.), Stress and human performance (pp. 49-88). Mahwah, NJ: Lawrence Erlbaum Associates.
12. Hockey, G. R., Maule, A. J., Vlough, P. J., and Bdzola, L. (2000). Effects of negative mood states on risk in everyday decision making. Cognition and Emotion, 14, 823-856.
13. Shaw, J. B., and Weekley, J. A. (1985). The effects of objective work-load variations of psychological strain and post-work-load performance. Journal of Management, 11, 87-98.
14. Searle, B. J., Bright, J. E. H., and Bochner, S. (1999). Testing the 3-factor model of occupational stress: the impact of demands, control and social support on a mail sorting task. Work and Stress, 13, 268-279.
15. Spector, P. E., Dwyer, D. J., and Jex, S. M. (1988). Relation of job stressors to affective, health, and performance outcomes: A comparison of multiple data sources. Journal of Applied Psychology, 73, 11-19.
16. Beehr, T. A., Jex, S. M., Stacy, B. A., and Murray, M. A. (2000). Work stressors and co-worker support as predictors of individual strain and job performance. Journal of Organizational Behaviour, 21, 391-405.
17. Andrews, F. M., and Farris, G. F. (1972). Time pressure and performance of scientists and engineers: A five-year panel study. Organizational Behaviour and Human Performance, 8, 185-200.
18. Jones, J. W., Barge, B. N., Steffy, B. D., Fay, L. M., Kunz, L. K., and Wuebker, L. J. (1988). Stress and medical malpractice: Organizational risk assessment and intervention. Journal of Applied Psychology, 73, 727-735.
19. Jackson, S. E., and Schuler, R. S. (1985). A meta-analysis and conceptual critique of research on role ambiguity and role conflict in work settings. Organizational Behaviour and Human Performance, 33, 1-21.
20. Tubbs, T. C., and Collins, J. M. (2000). Jackson and Schuler (1985) revisited: a meta-analysis of the relationships between role ambiguity, role conflict, and job performance. Journal of Management, 26, 155-169.
21. Jex, S. M. (1998). Stress and job performance: Theory, research, and implications for Managerial practice. Thousand Oaks, CA: Sage.

22. Westman, M., and Eden, D. (1996). The inverted-U relationship between stress and performance: a Field study. Work and Stress, 10, 165-173.
23. Payne, R. (1991). Individual differences in cognition and the stress process. In C. L. Cooper and R. Payne (eds.), Personality and stress: Individual differences in the stress process (pp. 181-204). New York: Wiley.
24. Jamal, M. (1985). Relationship of job stress to job performance: A study of managers and blue Collar workers. Human Relations, 38, 409-424.
25. Jex, S. M. (1998). Stress and job performance: Theory, research, and implications for managerial practice. Thousand Oaks, CA: Sage.
26. Kjellberg, A., Sköldström, B., Andersson, O., and Lindberg, L. (1996). Fatigue effects of noise on aeroplane mechanics. Work and Stress, 10, 62-71.
27. Sperandio, J. C. (1971). Variation of operator's strategies and regulating effects on workload. Ergonomics, 14, 571-577.
28. Hockey, G. R. J. (2000). Work environments and performance. In N. Chmiel (ed.), Work and organizational psychology: a European perspective (pp. 206-230). Oxford: Blackwell.
29. Klein, G. (1996). The effect of acute stressors on decision making. In J. E. Driskell and E. Salas (eds.), Stress and human performance (pp. 49-88). Mahwah, NJ: Lawrence Erlbaum Associates.
30. Motowidlo, S. J., Packard, J. S., and Manning, M. R. (1986). Occupational stress: Its causes and consequences on job performance. Journal of Applied Psychology, 71, 618-629.
31. Ibid.
32. Fay, D., and Sonnentag, S. (2001). Stressors and personal initiative: A study on organizational behaviour. Manuscript submitted for publication, Stress in Organizations.
33. Bunce, D., and West, M. (1994). Changing work environments: innovative coping responses to occupational stress. Work and Stress, 8, 319-331.
34. Spector, B. and Beer, M. (1994) Beyond TQM programmes, Journal of Organizational Change Management, 7, 2, 63-70.
35. Hackman, J. R. and Wageman, R. (1995) Total quality management: Empirical, conceptual and practical issues. *Administrative Science Quarterly*, 40, 309-342.

36. Deming, Edwards, W. (1986), *Out of the Crisis*, Cambridge, Massachusetts Institute of Technology, Centre for Advanced Engineering Study.
37. Juran, J. (1989), *Juran on Leadership for Quality*, New York, Free Press.
38. Buzzell, R. D. and Gale, B. T. (1987) The PIMS Principles: Linking Strategy to Performance, New York, Free Press.
39. Ibid.
40. Lawler, E.D., S.A Mohrman and E. Ledford Jr. (1998) *Strategies for High* Performance Organizations: Employee Involvement, TQM and Reengineering Programs in Fortune 1000 Corporations, San Francisco, Jossey-Bass.
41. Hendricks, K. B. and Singhal, V. (1997) Does implementing an effective TQM program actually improve operating performance? Empirical evidence from firms that have won quality awards. *Management Science*, 43, 1258-1274.
42. Hendricks, K. B. and Singhal, V. (2001) The long-run stock price performance of firms with effective TQM programs. Management Science, 47, 359-368.
43. Ernst and Young and American Quality Foundation (1992), The international quality study: *The* definitive study of the best international quality management practices: top-line findings, Ernest and Young, Cleveland, OH.
44. Kelly, K. (1992), Quality: Small and midsize companies seize the challenge–not a moment too soon, *Business Week*, 30, 66-99.
45. Beer, M., Eisenstat, R. A. and Spector, B. (1990) Why change program do not produce change, Harvard Business Review, November-December 1990.
46. Schaffer, R. H. (1998) The breakthrough strategy: Using short term success to build the high performance organization, Cambridge, Ballinger Publishing.
47. Zbaracki, M. J. (1998) The rhetoric and reality of total quality management," *Administrative* Science Quarterly, 43, 602-638.
48. K. Sridhara Bhat (2005): Total Quality Management, Text and Cases, Himalaya Publishing House, pp. 4-5.
49. Asthana, H.S. (1983). The Concept of Stress: A Phenomenological Approach; Paper presented at the seminar on stress, anxiety and mental health, University of Allahabad.
50. Srivastava, A. K. (1991). A study of role stress-mental health relationship as moderated by adopted coping strategies.

Psychological Studies, 36 (3), 192-197.

51. Easterbrook, J. A., "The Effect of Emotion on Cue Utilization and Organization of Behaviour," *Psychological Review*, Vol. 66, 1959, pp. 183-201.
52. Janis, I., and L. Mann, *Decision Making,* New York: The Free Press, 1977. Jex, S., *Stress and Job Performance*, Thousand Oaks, Calif.: Sage Publications, 1998.
53. Shaham, Y., J. Singer, and M. Schaeffer, "Stability/Instability of Cognitive Strategies Across Tasks Determine Whether Stress Will Affect Judgmental Processes," *Journal of Applied Psychology*, Vol. 22, No. 9, 1992, pp. 691-713.
54. Klein, G., "The Effects of Acute Stressors on Decision-Making," in J. Driskell and E. Salas, eds., *Stress and Human Performance*, Hillsdale, N.J.: Lawrence Erlbaum Associates, 1996, pp. 49-88.
55. Friedman, I. A., and L. Mann, "Coping Patterns in Adolescent Decision-Making: An Israeli-Australian Comparison," *Journal of Adolescence,* Vol. 16, 1993, pp. 187-199.
56. Keinan, G., "Decision-Making Under Stress: Scanning of Alternatives Under Controllable and Uncontrollable Threats," *Journal of Personalityand Social Psychology,* Vol. 52, No. 3, 1987, pp. 639-644.
57. Larsen, R., "Decision-Making by Military Students Under Extreme Stress," *Military Psychology*, Vol. 13, No. 2, 2001, pp. 89-92.
58. Idzikowski, C., and A. D. Baddeley, "Fear and Dangerous Environments," in R. Hockey, ed., *Stress and Fatigue in Human Performance*, Chichester, N.Y.: Wiley, 1983, pp. 123-144.
59. McLeod, P., "A Dual Task Modality Effect: Support for Multiprocessor Models of Attention," *Quarterly Journal of Experimental Psychology*, Vol. 29, No. 4, November 1977, pp. 651-667.
60. Driskell, J., R. Carson, and P. Moskal, *Stress and Human Performance: Final Report*, Orlando,
61. Fla.: Naval Training Systems Centre, August 15, 1988.
62. Janis, I., and L. Mann, *Decision Making,* New York: The Free Press, 1977.
63. Cropanzano, R., D. Rapp, and Z. Byrne, "The Relationship of Emotional Exhaustion to Work Attitudes, Job Performance, and Organizational Citizenship Behaviours," *Journal of Applied Psychology*, Vol. 88, No. 1, February 2003, pp. 160-169.

64. Goldberg, R.J. and Novack, D.H. (1992) The psychosocial review of systems. Social Science and Medicine, Vol. 35, No. 3, pp. 261- 269.
65. Surtees P.G. and Wainwright N.W.J (1998) Adversity over the life course: assessment and quantification issues. Stress Medicine, Vol. 14, No. 4, pp. 205-211.
66. Op cit p.7.
67. Holmes, T. H., and Rahe, R. H. (1967) The Social Readjustment Rating Scale. Journal of Psychosomatic Research, 11, 213-218.
68. Dohrenwend, B. S., and Dohrenwend, B. P. (1974) Stressful Life Events: Their Nature and Effects. Wiley and Sons, New York. Dohrenwend, B. S., Krasnoff, L., Askenasy, A. R., and Dohrenwend, B. P. (1988) The Psychiatric Epidemiology Research Interview Life Events Scale. In: L. Goldberg and S. Breznitz (eds.) Handbook of Stress: Theoretical and Clinical Aspects. Free Press, New York.
69. Fisher, S. (1996) Life change, personal control and disease. South African Journal of Psychology, Vol. 26, No. 1, pp. 16-22.
70. Perkins, D. V. (1988) The assessment of stress using life events scales. In: L. Gold-berg and S. Breznitz (eds.) Handbook of Stress: Theoretical and Clinical Aspects. Free Press, New York.
71. Rahe, R. H. (1969) Multi-cultural correlations of life change scaling: America, Japan, Denmark, and Sweden. Journal of Psychosomatic Research, 13, 191-195.
72. Abel, T.M., Metraux, R., and Roll, S. (1987) Psychotherapy and Culture, University of New Mexico Press, Albunquerque.
73. Tiblao, T.A. Work motivation and productivity of Government workers. Philippine Journal of Psychology (1990), Vol. 23, 30-38.
74. Orpen, C. Interactive effects of work motivation and personal control on employee job performance and satisfaction. Journal of Social Psychology (1994), Vol. 134 (6), 855-856.
75. Furnham, A., Forde, L., and Ferrari, K. Personality and work motivation. Personality and Individual Differences (1999), Vol. 26 (6), 1035-1043.
76. Knoop, R. Reliving stress through value-rich work. Journal of Social Psychology. (1994a) 134, 829-836.
77. Knoop, R. Work values and job satisfaction. Journal of Psychology (1994b) 128. 683-690.
78. Schein, E. H. (1992) *Organizational culture and leadership*, San

Francisco, Jossey-Bass.

79. Schein, E. H. (1992) *Organizational culture and leadership*, San Francisco, Jossey-Bass.
80. Spector, B. and Beer, M. (1994) Beyond TQM programmes, Journal of Organizational Change Management, 7, 2, 63-70.
81. Op cit, p. 14.
82. Miller, D. and Hartwick, J. (2002) Administrative fads and their paradoxical properties, Unpublished paper.
83. Op cit, p. 16.
84. Schaffer, R. H. (1998) The breakthrough strategy: Using short term success to build the high performance organization, Cambridge, Ballinger Publishing.
85. Ibid.
86. DiMaggio, P.J. and W. W. Powel (1983) "The iron cage revisited: Institutional isomorphism and collective rationality in organizational field," *American Sociological Review*, 48, 147-160.
87. Staw, B.M. and L.D. Epstein (2000) What bandwagons bring: Effects of popular management techniques on corporate performance, reputation and CEO pay, *Administrative Science Quarterly*, 45, 523-556.
88. Westphal, J.D., Gulati, R. and Shortell, S. M. (1997) Customization or conformity? An institutional and network perspective on the content and consequences of TQM adoptions, *Administrative Science Quarterly*, 42, 366-394.
89. Argyris, C. (1990) *Overcoming organizational defences*, Needham Heights, MA, Allyn, Bacon.
90. Beer, M. and Eisenstat, R. A. (2000) The silent killers of strategy implementation and learning, Sloan Management Review, 41, 4, 29-40.
91. Morrison, E. W. and Milliken, F. J. (2000) Organizational silence: A barrier to change and development in a pluralistic world, *Academy of Management Review*, 25, 4, 706-725.
92. Ibid.
93. Mallinger, M. as reported in Argyris, C. and Schon, D. A, (1993) *Organizational learning II: theory, method and practice*, Reading, MA, Addison Wesley.
94. Murphy, L.R., Hurrell, J.J. and Quick, J.C. (1992) Work and well-being: where do we go from here? In J.C. Quick, L.R. Murphy, and J.J. Hurrell (eds) Stress and Well-being at Work:

Assessments and Interventions for Occupational Mental Health. American Psychological Association, Washington DC.

95. Landy, F. J. (1992) Work design and stress. In: G. P. Keita and S. L. Sauter (eds) Work and Well-Being: An Agenda for the 1990s. American Psychological Association, Washington DC.
96. Murphy, L.R. (1988) Workplace interventions for stress reduction and prevention. In CL Cooper and R. Payne (Eds) Causes, Coping and Consequences of Stress at Work.
97. Van der Hek, H. and Plomp, H.N. (1997) Occupational stress management programmes: a practical overview of published effect studies. Occupational Medicine, 47 (3), 133-141.
98. Rosenstock, L. (1997) Work organization research at the National Institute for Occupational Safety and Health. Journal of Occupational Health Psychology, 2(1), 7-100.
99. Cox, T. (1988a) Psychobiological factors in stress and health. In S. Fisher and J. Reason (eds.) Handbook of Life Stress, Cognition and Health. Wiley and Sons, Chichester.

References

Abel, T.M., Metraux, R., and Roll, S.(1987) Psychotherapy and Culture, University of New Mexico Press, Albunquerque.

Argyris, C. (1990) *Overcoming organizational defences*, Needham Heights, MA, Allyn, Bacon.

Assessment of Operational Stress and Adaptive Coping Mechanisms of Soldiers, Washington, D.C.: Walter Reed.

Asthana, H.S.(1983). The Concept of Stress: A Phenomenological Approach; Paper presented at the seminar on stress, anxiety and mental health, University of Allahabad.

Beehr, T. A., Jex, S. M., Stacy, B. A., and Murray, M. A. (2000). Work stressors and co-worker support as predictors of individual strain and job performance. Journal of Organizational Behaviour, 21, 391-405.

Beer, M. and Eisenstat, R.A. (2000) The silent killers of strategy implementation and learning, Sloan Management Review, 41,4, 29-40.

Beer, M., Eisenstat, R.A. and Spector, B. (1990) Why change program do not produce change, Harvard Business Review, November-December. 1990.

Bunce, D., and West, M. (1994). Changing work environments: innovative coping responses to occupational stress. Work and

Stress, 8, 319-331.

Buzzell, R.D. and Gale, B.T. (1987) The PIMS Principles: Linking Strategy to Performance, New York, Free Press.

Campbell, MAJ S., CPT D. Ritzer, SGT J. Valentine, and COL R. Gifford, *Operation Joint Guard*, Bosnia: *An*

Clinical Aspects. Free Press, New York.

Cox, T. (1988a) Psychobiological factors in stress and health. In S. Fisher and J. Reason (eds.) Handbook of Life Stress, Cognition and Health. Wiley and Sons, Chichester.

Cropanzano, R., D. Rapp, and Z. Byrne, "The Relationship of Emotional Exhaustion to Work Attitudes, Job Performance, and Organizational Citizenship Behaviours," *Journal of Applied Psychology*, Vol. 88, No. 1, February 2003, pp. 160-169.

Deming, Edwards, W. (1986), *Out of the Crisis*, Cambridge, Massachusetts Institute of Technology, Centre for Advanced Engineering Study.

DiMaggio, P.J. and W.W. Powel (1983) "The iron cage revisited: Institutional isomorphism and collective rationality in organizational field," *American Sociological Review*, 48, 147-160.

Dohrenwend, B. S., Krasnoff, L., Askenasy, A. R., and Dohrenwend, B. P. (1988) The Psychiatric Epidemiology

Dohrenwend, B. S., and Dohrenwend, B. P. (1974) Stressful Life Events: Their Nature and Effects. Wiley and Sons, New York. 2001, pp. 89-92.

Driskell, J., R. Carson, and P. Moskal, *Stress and Human Performance: Final Report*, Orlando, Fla.: Naval Training Systems Centre, August 15, 1988.

Easterbrook, J.A., "The Effect of Emotion on Cue Utilization and Organization of Behaviour," *Psychological Review*, Vol. 66, 1959, pp. 183-201.

Ernst and Young and American Quality Foundation (1992), The international quality study: *The* definitive study of the best international quality management practices: top-line findings, Ernest and Young, Cleveland, OH.

Fay, D., and Sonnentag, S. (2001). Stressors and personal initiative: A study on organizational behaviour. Manuscript submitted for publication, Stress in Organizations.

Fisher, S. (1996) Life change, personal control and disease. South African Journal of Psychology, Vol. 26, No. 1, pp. 16-22.

Friedman, I.A., and L. Mann, "Coping Patterns in Adolescent Decision-Making: An Israeli-Australian Comparison," *Journal of Adolescence,* Vol. 16, 1993, pp. 187-199.

Furnham, A., Forde, L., and Ferrari, K. Personality and work motivation. Personality and Individual Differences (1999), Vol.26(6), 1035-1043.

Goldberg, R.J. and Novack, D.H. (1992) The psychosocial review of systems. Social Science andMedicine, Vol. 35, No. 3, pp. 261-269.

Hackman, J.R. and Wageman, R. (1995) Total quality management: Empirical, conceptual and practical issues. *Administrative Science Quarterly*, 40, 309-342.

Halverson, CPT R., CPT P. Bliese, SGT R. Moore, and CPT C. Castro, *Psychological Well-Being and Physical Health Symptoms Deployed for Operation Uphold Democracy*: A Summary of Human Dimensions Research in Haiti, Washington, D.C.: Walter Reed Army Institute for Research, 1995.

Hayes, Treasa (1997) The Learning Organisation: Fashionable Fad or Path to Progress?

Hendricks, K.B. and Singhal, V. (1997) Does implementing an effective TQM program actually improve operating performance? Empirical evidence from firms that have won quality awards. *Management Science*, 43, 1258-1274.

Hendricks, K.B. and Singhal, V. (2001) The long-run stock price performance of firms with effective TQM programs. Management Science, 47, 359-368.

Hockey, G. R. J. (2000). Work environments and performance. In N. Chmiel (Ed.), Work and organizational psychology: a European perspective (pp. 206-230). Oxford: Blackwell.

Hockey, G.R., Maule, A.J., Vlough, P.J., and Bdzola, L. (2000). Effects of negative mood states on risk in everyday decision making. Cognition and Emotion, 14, 823-856.

Holmes, T.H., and Rahe, R.H. (1967) The Social Readjustment Rating Scale. Journal of Psychosomatic Research, 11, 213-218.

Idzikowski, C., and A.D. Baddeley, "Fear and Dangerous Environments," in R. Hockey, ed., *Stress and Fatigue in Human Performance*, Chichester, N.Y.: Wiley, 1983, pp. 123-144.

Jackson, S.E., and Schuler, R.S. (1985). A meta-analysis and conceptual critique of research on role ambiguity and role conflict in work settings. Organizational Behaviour and Human

Performance, 33, 1-21.

Jamal, M. (1985). Relationship of job stress to job performance: A study of managers and blue Collar workers.

Janis, I., and L. Mann, *Decision Making*, New York: The Free Press, 1977.Jex, S., *Stress and Job Performance*, Thousand Oaks, Calif.: Sage Publications, 1998.

Janis, I., and L. Mann, *Decision Making*, New York: The Free Press, 1977.

Jex, S. M. (1998). Stress and job performance: Theory, research, and implications for Managerial practice. Thousand Oaks, CA: Sage.

Jex, S. M. (1998). Stress and job performance: Theory, research, and implications for managerial practice. Thousand Oaks, CA: Sage.

Jones, J.W., Barge, B.N., Steffy, B.D., Fay, L.M., Kunz, L.K., and Wuebker, L.J. (1988). Stress and medical malpractice: Organizational risk assessment and intervention. Journal of Applied Psychology, 73, 727-735.

Journal of Occupational Health Psychology, 2(1), 7-100.

Juran, J. (1989), *Juran on Leadership for Quality*, New York, Free Press.

K. Sridhara Bhat (2005): Total Quality Management, Text and Cases, Himalaya Publishing House, pp 4-5.

Keinan, G., "Decision-Making Under Stress: Scanning of Alternatives Under Controllable and Uncontrollable Threats," *Journal of Personalityand Social Psychology*, Vol. 52, No. 3, 1987, pp. 639-644.

Kelly, K. (1992), Quality: Small and midsize companies seize the challenge–not a moment too soon, *Business Week*, 30, 66-99.

Kjellberg, A., Sköldström, B., Andersson, O., and Lindberg, L. (1996). Fatigue effects of noise on aeroplane mechanics. Work and Stress, 10, 62-71.

Klein, G. (1996). The effect of acute stressors on decision making. In J. E. Driskell and E. Salas (Eds.), Stress and human performance (pp. 49-88). Mahwah, NJ: Lawrence Erlbaum Associates.

Klein, G. (1996). The effect of acute stressors on decision making. In J. E. Driskell and E. Salas (Eds.), Stress and human performance (pp. 49-88). Mahwah, NJ: Lawrence Erlbaum Associates.

Klein, G., "The Effects of Acute Stressors on Decision-Making," in J. Driskell and E. Salas, eds., *Stress and Human Performance*, Hillsdale, N.J.: Lawrence Erlbaum Associates, 1996, pp. 49-88.

Knoop., R. Reliving stress through value-rich work. Journal of Social

Psychology. (1994a) 134, 829-836.

Knoop., R. Work values and job satisfaction. Journal of Psychology (1994b) 128. 683-690.

Landy, F. J. (1992) Work design and stress. In: G. P. Keita and S. L. Sauter (eds.) Work and Well-Being: An Agenda for the 1990s. American Psychological Association, Washington DC.

Larsen, R., "Decision-Making by Military Students Under Extreme Stress," *Military Psychology*, Vol. 13, No. 2,

Lawler, E.D., S.A Mohrman and E. Ledford Jr. (1998) *Strategies for High* PerformanceOrganizations: Employee Involvement, TQM and Reengineering Programs in Fortune 1000 Corporations, San Francisco, Jossey-Bass.

Mallinger, M. as reported in Argyris, C. and Schon, D. A, (1993) *Organizational learning II: theory, method and*

McLeod, P., "A Dual Task Modality Effect: Support for Multiprocessor Models of Attention," *Quarterly Journal of Experimental Psychology*, Vol. 29, No. 4, November 1977, pp. 651-667.

Miller, D. and Hartwick, J. (2002) Administrative fads and their paradoxical properties, Unpublished paper.

Morrison, E. W. and Milliken, F. J. (2000) Organizational silence: A barrier to change and development in a pluralistic world, *Academy of Management Review*, 25, 4, 706-725.

Motowidlo, S. J., Packard, J. S., and Manning, M. R. (1986). Occupational stress: Its causes and consequences on job performance. Journal of Applied Psychology, 71, 618-629.

Murphy, L.R. (1988) Workplace interventions for stress reduction and prevention. In CL Cooper and R. Payne (eds.) Causes, Coping and Consequences of Stress at Work.

Murphy, L.R., Hurrell, J.J. and Quick, J.C. (1992) Work and well-being: where do we go from here? In J.C. Quick, L.R. Murphy, and J.J. Hurrell (eds) Stress and Well-being at Work: Assessments and Interventions for Occupational Mental Health. American Psychological Association, Washington DC.

Orpen., C. Interactive effects of work motivation and personal control on employee job performance and satisfaction. Journal of Social Psychology (1994), Vol. 134 (6), 855-856.

Payne, R. (1991). Individual differences in cognition and the stress process. In C. L. Cooper and R. Payne (Eds.), Personality and stress: Individual differences in the stress process (pp. 181-204).

New York: Wiley.

Perkins, D.V. (1988) The assessment of stress using life events scales. In: L. Gold-berg and S. Breznitz (eds.) Handbook of Stress: Theoretical and Clinical Aspects. Free Press, New York.

Postman, L., and Bruner, J.S. (1948). Perception under stress. Psychological Review, 55, 314-323.

Rahe, R.H. (1969) Multi-cultural correlations of life change scaling: America, Japan, Denmark, and Sweden. Journal of Psychosomatic Research, 13, 191-195.

Raju Arisetti: Stress Strikes Corporate World, *Economic Times Esquire*, October, 28, 1989, p.1.

Research Interview Life Events Scale. In: L. Goldberg and S. Breznitz (eds.) Handbook of Stress: Theoretical and

Rosenstock, L. (1997) Work organization research at the National Institute for Occupational Safety and Health.

Schaffer, R.H. (1998) The breakthrough strategy: Using short term success to build the high performance organization, Cambridge, Ballinger Publishing.

Schaffer, R.H. (1998) The breakthrough strategy: Using short term success to build the high performance organization, Cambridge, Ballinger Publishing.

Schein, E.H. (1992) *Organizational culture and leadership*, San Francisco, Jossey-Bass.

Searle, B.J., Bright, J.E.H., and Bochner, S. (1999). Testing the 3-factor model of occupational stress: the impact of demands, control and social support on a mail sorting task. Work and Stress, 13, 268-279.

Selye, H. The Stress of Life, New York: McGraw-Hill, 1956.

Shaham, Y., J. Singer, and M. Schaeffer, "Stability/Instability of Cognitive Strategies Across Tasks Determine

Shaw, J.B., and Weekley, J.A. (1985). The effects of objective work-load variations of psychological strain and post-work-load performance. Journal of Management, 11, 87-98.

Spector, B. and Beer, M. (1994) Beyond TQM programmes, Journal of Organizational Change Management, 7, 2, 63-70.

Spector, B. and Beer, M. (1994) Beyond TQM programmes, Journal of Organizational Change Management, 7, 2, 63-70.

Spector, P.E., Dwyer, D.J., and Jex, S.M. (1988). Relation of job stressors to affective, health, and performance

Sperandio, J.C. (1971). Variation of operator's strategies and regulating effects on workload. Ergonomics, 14, 571-577.

Srivastava, A.K.. (1991). A study of role stress-mental health relationship as moderated by adopted coping strategies. Psychological Studies, 36 (3), 192-197.

Staw, B.M. and L.D. Epstein (2000) What bandwagons bring: Effects of popular management techniques on corporate performance, reputation and CEO pay, *Administrative Science Quarterly*, 45, 523-556.

Surtees P.G. and Wainwright N.W.J (1998) Adversity over the life course: assessment and quantification issues. Stress Medicine, vol. 14, no. 4, pp. 205-211.

Tiblao., T.A. Work motivation and productivity of Government workers. Philippine Journal of Psychology (1990), Vol.23, 30-38.

Tubbs, T.C., and Collins, J. M. (2000). Jackson and Schuler (1985) revisited: a meta-analysis of the relationships between role ambiguity, role conflict, and job performance. Journal of Management, 26, 155-169.

Van der Hek, H. and Plomp, H.N. (1997) Occupational stress management programmes: a practical overview of published effect studies. Occupational Medicine, 47 (3), 133-141.

Virginia M. Gibson: Stress in Work Place: A Hidden Cost Factor,H.R.Focus,January,1993, p.15.

Westman, M., and Eden, D. (1996). The inverted-U relationship between stress and performance: a Field study. Work and Stress, 10, 165-173.

Westphal, J.D., Gulati, R. and Shortell, S. M. (1997) Customization or conformity? An institutional and network perspective on the content and consequences of TQM adoptions, *Administrative Science Quarterly*, 42, 366-394.

Whether Stress Will Affect Judgmental Processes," *Journal of Applied Psychology*, Vol. 22, No. 9, 1992, pp. 691-692.

World Health Organization (2003). Authored by: Cassitto, M.G., Fattorini, E., Gilioni, R., Rengo, C. and Gonik, V. 'Raising Awareness of Psychological Harassment at Work'. Geneva: WHO, 2003 (Protecting Workers' Health series No. 4). Geneva: WHO.

World Health Organization (2004). Authored by: Leka, S., Griffiths, A. and Cox, T. Work Organization and Stress: Systematic problem approaches for employers, managers and trade unions representatives. Geneva: WHO (Protecting Workers' Health series 3). Geneva: World Health Organization (WHO).

Zbaracki, M.J. (1998) The rhetoric and reality of total quality management," *Administrative* Science Quarterly, 43, 602-638.

4

Impact of Stress on TQM

4.1 *Good* Stress

Although much of the research on the relationship between stress and functioning focuses on the negative performance effects of stress, not all stress is bad. In fact, Selye (1956) [1] emphasizes that stress is a necessary part of life and that it does not always involve negative consequences for the organism involved. In fact, at certain moderate levels, stress can actually improve individual performance. There is substantial research supporting the concept of "good stress." Yerkes and Dodson (1908) [2] were the first to "stumble" upon the inverted-U relationship between stress and performance. Their work focused on the effects of stress on the learning response of rats. Using three trials with low, moderate, and high levels of stimulus, the authors find a weak but curvilinear relationship, with performance on the task improving as the stressor stimulus reached a moderate level and decreasing as stimulus strength increased beyond this point.

Research since Yerkes and Dodson has supported the inverted-U relationship between stress and performance. Scott (1966) [3] finds that individual performance increases with stress and resulting arousal to an optimal point and then decreases as stress and stimulation increase beyond this optimum. Furthermore, Srivastava and Krishna (1991) [4] find evidence that an inverted-U relationship does exist for job performance in the industrial context. Selye (1975) [5] and McGrath (1976) [6] also suggest an inverted-U relationship between stress and performance.

Finally, research on arousal theory supports the inverted-U hypothesis, assuming that external stressors produce a stress response that is similar physiologically to arousal. Sanders

(1983) [7] and Gaillard and Steyvers (1989) [8] find that performance is optimal when arousal is at moderate levels. When arousal is either too high or too low, performance declines. Although several authors posit a negative linear relationship between stress and performance, other evidence suggests that this relationship is actually an inverted-U shape. This hypothesis suggests that individual performance on a given task will be lower at high and low levels of stress and optimal at moderate levels of stress. At moderate levels of stress, performance is likely to be improved by the presence of enough stimulation to keep the individual vigilant and alert, but not enough to divert or absorb his energy and focus. At low levels of stress, in contrast, activation and alertness may be too low to foster effective performance, while at high levels of stress; arousal is too high to be conducive to task performance.

The relationship between pressure and performance is explained in one of the oldest and most important ideas in stress management, the "Inverted-U" relationship between pressure and performance (see below). The Inverted-U relationship focuses on people's performance of a task.

When there is very little pressure on us to carry out an important task, there is little incentive for us to focus energy and attention on it. This is particularly the case when there may be other, more urgent, or more interesting, tasks competing for attention. As pressure on us increases, we enter the "area of best performance". Here, we are able to focus on the task and perform well–there is enough pressure on us to focus our attention but not so much that it disrupts our performance.

There are many critics of the inverted-U hypothesis who argue that the relationship between stress and performance does not have a U-shape. One alternative model is a negative linear relationship. Jamal (1985) [9] argues that stress at any level reduces task performance by draining an individual's energy, concentration, and time. Vroom (1964) [10] offers a similar explanation, suggesting that physiological responses caused by stressors impairs performance. Some psychologists even suggest a linear positive relationship between stress and performance. For example, Meglino (1977) [11] argues that at low levels of stress, challenge is absent and performance is poor. Optimal performance in his model comes at the highest level of stress.

There have been some studies in support of this hypothesis, including Arsenault and Dolan (1983) [12] and Hatton (1995) [13]. Despite the empirical evidence supporting these alternative theories, the inverted-U hypothesis is still the most intuitively appealing and the most used explanation for how stress and performance are related (Muse, Harris, and Field, 2003) [14].

4.2 Stress and Performance

When stress is too low a person may be under stimulated resulting in boredom, poor motivation and low levels of activity. As stress increases, it may help a person perform at their optimal level. When stress rises above a certain level performance becomes impaired. If stress continues to increase, performance is likely to deteriorate. It is important to become aware of the optimal stress level and work at maintaining it.

The stress process begins with environmental demand. The environment influences a person towards his attitude and behaviour. The physical and psychological response due to environment gets the root for the stress in the stage 1.

In stage 2 the amount of threat is perceived by the individual physically and psychologically. Due to perceiving of threat the stress starts responding physically and psychologically. If the threat involves then stress would arise.

In stage 3 the stress response clearly seen. Due toe stress arousal, state of anxiety, muscle tension and changes in attention would take place. The stress can be seen clearly at this stage. With physical and psychological response of stress even sweating will increase on palms.

In stage 4 the behavioural consequences can be seen clearly. The performance or outcome would take place with stress. The performance or outcome is depended upon the amount of stress or level of stress. If the stress level is beyond the manageable level, the performance can be declined but if the stress level is suitable for performance, it increases the performance.

4.3 Stress and Job Satisfaction

Research also suggests that moderate levels of stress can have positive effects on job satisfaction and organizational commitment while reducing turnover intent. These findings seem to be an extension of the inverted-U-shaped relationship discussed previously. Under this hypothesis, at moderate levels of stress, individual performance and productivity are likely to be higher and can also contribute to higher job satisfaction and organizational commitment. Zivnuska, Kiewitz, and Hochwarter (2002) [15] find that moderate levels of stress tend to be correlated with higher levels of job satisfaction than either very high or very low stress levels.

There are stressors which are associated with organization itself. Although the organization is made up of groups of individuals, there are also more macro level dimensions, unique to the organization that contains potential sources. These macro level stressors can be categorized into administrative policies and strategies, organizational structure and design, organizational processes, and working conditions. Some specific examples of these organizational stressors include responsibility without authority, inability to voice complaints, inadequate recognition, and lack of clear job description or reporting relationships. It should be noted that as organizations dramatically change to meet the environmental challenges, there are more and more accompanying stressors for individual employees in their jobs.

Although stress is a physiological response to external stimuli, the stress response can also affect individuals in many important dimensions beyond simple physiological reactions. For example, individual and group performance, decision making processes, and perception are all affected by stressors. Because operational deployments inherently have many stressors that may affect military personnel and their functioning, understanding each part of this framework is essential to improve the effectiveness of soldiers during deployments. In general, stress is considered to have an inverted U-shaped relationship with performance that is, performance may improve under moderate levels of stress but decline under high or constant stress.

Though few, if any, individuals are likely to be completely immune to the effects of stress on performance, there are intervening variables, known as moderators that can reduce the performance decrement caused by stress. A moderator variable is one that affects the relationship between the independent and dependent variables, usually decreasing the causal relationship between the two. Although moderators usually reduce the effect of stress on performance, there are moderators that can have the opposite effect and actually increase the performance effects of stress. Moderators come in a variety of forms, ranging from personality type to specifically targeted forms of training.

Although this framework divides moderators into two categories, it is worth noting that some moderators may function as both type 1 and type 2 moderators, depending on the context. For example, training can help to reduce the physiological stress response to an external stressor and also prevent performance degradation in the face of stress. For cases in which moderators could be both types, the author classified each moderator into what appears to be the most common manifestation of the moderator.

Stress in organizations may not only impact individual health and well-being but also performance. Performance refers to individuals' actions that are relevant for organizational goals (Campbell, McCloy, Oppler, and Sager,

1993) [16]. Borman and Motowidlo (1993) [17] differentiated between task and contextual performance. Task performance refers to in-role behaviours which contribute to the organization's 'technical core'. Contextual performance refers to extra-role, discretionary behaviours which do not directly contribute to an organization's technical core but which are assumed to support its broader organizational, social, and psychological environment.

4.4 Stress and Decision-making

Stress can affect an individual's decision-making process and ability to make effective judgments. For example, Easterbrook (1959) [18] proposes a "cue utilization model" and argues that when exposed to stressors, individuals experience "perceptual narrowing"-meaning that they pay attention to fewer perceptual cues or stimuli that could contribute to their behaviour or decision. Peripheral stimuli are likely to be the first to be screened out or ignored.

Decision making models proposed by Janis and Mann (1977) [19] support this hypothesis and suggest that under stress, individuals may make decisions based on incomplete information. Friedman and Mann (1993) [20] suggest that when under conditions of stress, individuals may fail to consider the full range of alternatives available, ignore long-term consequences, and make decisions based on oversimplifying assumptions. Furthermore, the work of Staw, Sandelands, and Dutton (1981) [21] suggests that individuals may suffer from performance rigidity as a result of their reduced search behaviour and reliance on fewer perceptual cues to make decisions.

Research by Shaham, Singer, and Schaeffer (1992) [22] suggests that individuals are more likely to use heuristics (rules of thumb or guidelines based on past experience that are used to help in decision making) when they are faced with external stressors. They compare the heuristic use of two groups of people on a survey, one that was asked to first complete an analytical test while being subjected to loud noises and a second that did not complete the stress-exposure test. These authors find that individuals in the experimental group, who exhibited elevated levels of hostility, anxiety, and irritability after their initial exposure to the stressors, were about 12.5 percent more likely than the control group to use heuristics while taking the second survey.

However, the authors do not look at whether individuals performed better or worse on the analytical test when using heuristics. Klein (1996) [23] also finds that when confronted with external stressors, individuals are more likely to use heuristics and other simplified decision making strategies. However, rather than reducing the quality of individual decisions, as suggested by those researchers who argue for perceptual narrowing, Klein suggests that the use of heuristics may allow individuals to respond more quickly to external demands and can also help them make effective judgments under some kinds of stressors or with only partial information.

Stress can also contribute to performance decrements by slowing cognition and individual information processing. Idzikowski and Baddeley (1983) [24] find that the time to complete a given task doubled with the introduction of an external stressor. McLeod (1977) [25] looks specifically at stress in the form of "task overload" (e.g., asking an individual to perform more than one task under a time constraint) and finds that the addition of multiple required tasks reduces the quality of individual performance and increases the magnitude of the performance decrement as compared with the case in which the individual has only one task to perform. While the affects of stress on individual performance are relevant to military effectiveness, the effects of stress on group functioning are equally important. Bowers, Weaver, and Morgan (1996) [26] argue that group-level stressors can involve any influence of the group on the individual that leads to increased tension or decreased functioning, competition among members or crowding. Group decision making processes can be affected by the presence of stressors.

Most importantly, Driskell, Carson, and Moskal (1988) [27] find that when subjected to stressful conditions, individuals are more likely to yield control to their partners or superiors. As a result, authority tends to become more concentrated and hierarchy more pronounced. In addition, communication within the group may suffer as a result of perceptual narrowing. Cannon-Bowers and Salas (1998) [28] hypothesize that the stimuli lost through perceptual narrowing are those most important to group communication and effectiveness. As a result, the group-level effects of stress may be even more significant than those at the individual level. Stress can also lead to what Janis and Mann (1977) [29] call "groupthink," in which members of the group may ignore important cues, force all members to conform or adhere to the consensus opinion, and even rationalize poor decisions.

The authors explain this effect by noting that moderate stress is perceived as stimulating and challenging, without being unbearable. Empirically, the authors demonstrate the nonlinear relationship of stress with turnover intent, value attainment, and job satisfaction by including a tension-squared term as a predictor variable in their model. They find that the tension-squared term has a statistically significant relationship with each of the outcome variables. These findings suggest that turnover intent increases quadratically with job tension, while value attainment and job satisfaction decrease quadratically with tension.

These findings are supported by the work of Milgram, Orenstein, and Zafrir (1989) [30], which looks at the effects of stress on a group of Israeli soldiers. They find that moderate levels of stress foster increased group cooperation, commitment, and morale, all of which can contribute to effective group performance. As stress levels decline from the "optimal" level, the authors find that individual endorsement of official goals of the military, military unit morale, and loyalty to the unit also decline. Taken together, these studies suggest that although stress often comes along with a negative connotation in popular language, it does exist in positive and helpful forms that can contribute to individual and group intensity and achievement. This type of stress is likely to be particularly important for military personnel in peacekeeping deployments, where a certain level of stress may help maintain vigilance and reduce boredom.

4.5 Assessing the Risk at Work

The experience or work stress is a challenge to the health and safety of workers and to the healthiness of their organisations. Employers should have a policy for the management of workers health that makes reference to work stress. They should enable that policy to be implemented by putting the appropriate arrangements in place. Such arrangements should address the issues of risk assessment, timely reaction and rehabilitation. Organisational level strategies for managing existing work stress focus on combating the risks at source.

Work stress can be effectively managed by applying a risk management approach as is successfully done with other major health and safety problems. A risk management approach assesses the possible risks in the work environment that may cause particular existing hazards to cause harm to employees. A hazard is an event or situation that has the potential for causing harm. Harm refers to physical or psychological deterioration of health. The causes of stress are hazards related to the design and management of work and working conditions, and such hazards can be managed and their effects controlled in the same way as other hazards.

4.6 Essential Steps in Risk Management

Risk management is essentially a problem solving approach to health and safety problems and provides a vehicle for the continuous improvement or work and working conditions and thus the health of workers and the healthiness of their organisations.

Risk management proceeds through a cycle of five actions

1. An analysis of the situation and an assessment of risk.
2. The design of an action plan to reduce the risk of work stress.
3. The implementation of that action plan and its evaluation.
4. Learning and further action based on the results of that evaluation.

Cox (2000) has also described a five-step strategy to carry out a risk assessment process in practice.

Each step builds on information collected during any preceding step. The initial steps (Steps 1, and 2) are designed to build a model of the work and working conditions of the assessment group that is good enough to support the design and later use of the assessment instrument (Step 3). This instrument is used to quantify the workers' exposure (at group level) to all the significant stressors associated with their work and working conditions, and assess their health.

The five steps are largely sequential with one possible exception. The Audit of Existing Management Control and Employee Support Systems (Step 4) can be conducted either in parallel with the Work Analysis Interviews, or following the Analysis and Interpretation of Assessment Data. It is often most convenient to conduct it in parallel with the Work Analysis Interviews. In this case, the information collected can usefully contribute to the working model of the assessment group's situation that is built up in the early stages of the assessment. Finally, all information is analysed and interpreted (Step 5).

Think about different work groups or workplaces that make up the organisation and a question is to be raised which is most stressed or stressful. The evidence is to be identified like high absence rates, poor health records, high accident rates, poor morale, workers or trade union complaints, poor productivity etc. The investigation is to be made in examining the working conditions.

Identification, collection and discussion of the evidences is to be done in the team manner apart from consulting the workers and trade unions possibly through group discussion. A proper plan of action is to be made and implemented in the relevant manner in order to overcome the stress conditions revision of action plan is to be done and implemented in order to overcome the risks in the organisations.

The complexity of the modern workplace and the constant changes are just a few of the reasons why organizations need to address the stress problem. If this reason is added to the legal and financial ramifications of not doing so it starts to become obvious that addressing stress in the work place is imperative. It would be incorrect to assume with particular references to stress, that the control element management has the sole responsibility.

Any culture change would primarily be through education, but could be greatly enhanced by an appropriate and competent mentoring system backed up by the proposed organizational culture of recognition and support. The five stages of team work are:

1. **Aware:** The team work can be developed through development of thoughts, ideas, feelings, values, data, intuition, conscious or subconscious.
2. **Accept:** In order to develop team work through this accept nature we can bring people to consciousness.
3. **Adopt:** The adoption is depended upon the gain. If it gains the employees through adoption can be taken into consideration.
4. **Adapt:** This relates to adapt the behaviour for getting results or benefits. The thoughts, feeling, and actions which are needed to change should be considered to gain benefit.
5. **Act:** This is the final stage in which change in thoughts, ideas, feelings and values leading to change in behaviour. The original outcome takes place at this stage.

Mangers of organizations have a dual perspective of stress.

Ultimately they have to develop work group effectiveness. The managers need to be aware of their own stress levels, as well as those of their subordinates. Most of the literature focuses on ways of reducing stress. However, a more appropriate approach might be to examine ways of optimizing stress. In many contests the stress is used as distress rather than eustress. As mentioned in the previous chapter French, Kast, and Rosenzweig (1985) [31] state that the challenge is to minimize distress and maintain eustress. They point out that the conditions of organizational life create a series of paradoxes that demonstrate the need for balance and equilibrium. In the organization if the stress levels are at the manageable level, the performance would be increased which leads to group effectiveness.

In the organization the role of management becomes one of maintaining an appropriate level of stress by providing an optimal environment, and "by doing a good job in areas such as performance planning, role analysis, work redesign/job enrichment, continuing feedback, ecological considerations, and interpersonal skills training." When appropriate level of training is given and involves the employees in the decision making with team spirit, it leads to group effectiveness. There are essentially three strategies for dealing with stress in organizations (Jick and Payne, 1980): (1) treat the symptoms, (2) change the person, and (3) remove the cause of the stress. When a person is already suffering from the effects of stress, the first priority is to treat the symptoms. This includes both the identification of those suffering from excessive stress, as well as providing health-care and psychological counselling services. The second approach is to help individuals build stress management skills to make them less vulnerable to its effects. Examples would be teaching employee's time management and relaxation techniques, or suggesting changes to one's diet or exercise. The third approach is to eliminate or reduce the environmental situation that is creating the stress. This would involve reducing environmental stressors such as noise and pollution, or modifying production schedules and work-loads.

Notes

1. Selye, H. (1956) Stress of Life. McGraw-Hill, New York.
2. Yerkes, R., and J. Dodson, "The Relation of Strength of Stimulus to Rapidity of Habit Formation," Journal of Comparative Neurology and Psychology, Vol. 18, 1908, pp. 459-482.
3. Scott, W.E., Jr., "Activation Theory and Task Design," *Organizational Behaviour and Human Performance,* No. 1, 1966, pp. 3-30.
4. Srivastava, A.K., and A. Krishna, "A Test of Inverted U Hypothesis of Stress Performance Relationship in the Industrial Context," *Psychological Studies*, Vol. 34, 1991, pp. 34-38.
5. Selye, H., *Stress without Distress,* New York: JP Lippicott Company, 1975.
6. McGrath, J.E., "Stress and Behaviour in Organizations," in M. D. Dunnette, ed., *Handbook of Industrial and Organizational Psychology: Vol. 3*, 2nd edition, Chicago: Rand McNally, 1976, pp. 1351-1395.
7. Sanders, A. F., "Towards a Model for Stress and Human Performance," *Acta Psychologica*, Vol. 53, 1983, pp. 61-97.
8. Gaillard, A.W.K., and F.J.M. Steyvers, "Sleep Loss and Sustained Performance," in A. Coblentz, ed., *Vigilance and Performance in Automatized Systems*, Dordrecht, The Netherlands: Kluwer Academic Publishers, 1989.
9. Jamal, M., "Relationship of Job Stress to Job Performance: A Study of Managers and Blue-Collar Workers," *Human Relations*, Vol. 38, 1985, pp. 409-424.
10. Vroom, V.H., *Work and Motivation,* New York: Wiley Press, 1964.
11. Meglino, B.M., "Stress and Performance: Are They Always Incompatible?" *Supervisory Management*, Vol. 22, No. 3, 1977, pp. 2-12.
12. Arsenault, A., and S. Dolan, "The Role of Personality, Occupation, and Organization in Understanding the Relationship Between Job Stress, Performance, and Absenteeism," *Journal of Occupational Psychology*, Vol. 56, 1983, pp. 227-240.
13. Hatton, C., et al., "Stressors, Coping Strategies, and Stress

Related Outcomes Among Direct Care Staff in Staffed Houses for People with Learning Disabilities," *Mental Handicap Research*, Vol. 8, 1995, pp. 252-271.

14. Muse, L., S. Harris, and H. Field, "Has the Inverted-U Theory of Stress and Job Performance Had a Fair Test?" *Human Performance,* Vol. 16, No. 4, September 2003, pp. 349-364.
15. Zivnuska, S., C. Kiewitz, and W. Hochwarter, "What Is Too Much or Too Little? The Curvilinear Effects of Job Tension on Turnover Intent, Value Attainment, and Job Satisfaction," *Journal of Applied Psychology*, Vol. 32, No. 7, July 2002, pp. 1334-1360.
16. Campbell, J.P., McCloy, R.A., Oppler, S.H., and Sager, C.E. (1993). A theory of performance. In E. Schmitt, W. C. Borman, and Associates (eds.), Personnel selection in organizations (pp. 35-70). San Francisco: Jossey-Bass.
17. Borman, W.C., and Motowidlo, S.J. (1993). Expanding the criterion domain to include elements of contextual performance. In N. Schmitt and W. Borman (Eds.), Personnel selection in organizations (pp. 71-98). New York: Jossey-Bass.
18. Easterbrook, J.A., "The Effect of Emotion on Cue Utilization and Organization of Behaviour," *Psychological Review*, Vol. 66, 1959, pp. 183-201.
19. Janis, I., and L. Mann, *Decision-Making,* New York: The Free Press, 1977.
20. Friedman, I.A., and L. Mann, "Coping Patterns in Adolescent Decision-Making: An Israeli-Australian Comparison," *Journal of Adolescence,* Vol. 16, 1993, pp. 187-199.
21. Staw, R.M., L.E. Sandelands, and J.E. Dutton, "Threat-Rigidity Effects in Organizational Behaviour: A Multi-Level Analysis," *Administrative Quarterly*, No. 26, 1981, pp. 501-524.
22. Shaham, Y., J. Singer, and M. Schaeffer, "Stability/Instability of Cognitive Strategies Across Tasks Determine Whether Stress Will Affect Judgmental Processes," *Journal of Applied Psychology*, Vol. 22, No. 9, 1992, pp. 691-713.
23. Klein, G., "The Effects of Acute Stressors on Decision-Making," in J. Driskell and E. Salas, eds., *Stress and Human Performance*, Hillsdale, N.J.: Lawrence Erlbaum Associates, 1996, pp. 49-88.
24. Idzikowski, C., and A.D. Baddeley, "Fear and Dangerous Environments," in R. Hockey, ed., *Stress and Fatigue in Human Performance*, Chichester, N.Y.: Wiley, 1983, pp. 123-144.

25. McLeod, P., "A Dual Task Modality Effect: Support for Multiprocessor Models of Attention," *Quarterly Journal of Experimental Psychology*, Vol. 29, No. 4, November 1977, pp. 651-667.
26. Bowers, C., J. Weaver, and B. Morgan, Jr., "Moderating the Performance Effects of Stress," in James Driskell and Eduardo Salas, eds., *Stress and Human Performance*, Hillsdale, N.J.: Lawrence Erlbaum Associates, 1996, pp. 163-192.
27. Driskell, J., R. Carson, and P. Moskal, *Stress and Human Performance: Final Report*, Orlando, Fla: Naval Training Systems Centre, August 15, 1988.
28. Cannon-Bowers, J., and E. Salas, "Individual and Team Decision-Making Under Stress: Theoretical Underpinnings," in J. Cannon-Bowers and E. Salas, eds., *Making Decisions Under Stress*, Washington, D.C.: American Psychological Association, 1998, pp. 17-37.
29. Janis, I., and L. Mann, *Decision Making*, New York: The Free Press, 1977.
30. Milgram, N., R. Orenstein, and E. Zafrir, "Stressors, Personal Resources, and Social Supports in Military Performance During Wartime," *Military Psychology*, Vol. 1, No. 4, 1989, pp. 185-199.
31. Ibid.

5

Case Studies

5.1 Importance of Case Study Method

A case study is one of several ways of doing research whether it is social science related or even socially related. It is an intensive study of a single group, incident, or community. [1] Other ways include experiments, surveys, multiple histories, and analysis of archival information. [2]

Rather than using samples and following a rigid protocol to examine limited number of variables, case study methods involve an in-depth, longitudinal examination of a single instance or event individual case. They provide a systematic way of looking at events, collecting data, analyzing information, and reporting the results. As a result the researcher may gain a sharpened understanding of why the instance happened as it did, and what might become important to look at more extensively in future research. Case studies lend themselves to both generating and testing hypotheses. [3]

The case study method [4] is considered as an effective device which portrays minute details of institutional functioning. Further, the case study method is a technique by which individual factor whether it can be an institution or just an episode in the life of an individual or a group is analysed in its relationship to any other in the group. [5] An authority has used the words "The Social Microscope" for the case study method. [6] Pauline V. Young describes case study as "a comprehensive study of social unit; be that unit a person, a group, a social institution, a district or a community. [7] Goode and Halt regard that case study is a way of organizing social data so as to preserve the unitary character of the social object being studies expressed somewhat differently, it is an which views any social unit as a whole. The approach include the development of unit, which may be a person or a family or other social group, a set of relationships or processes or even an entire culture. [8]

Another suggestion is that case study should be defined as a research strategy, an empirical inquiry that investigates a phenomenon within its real-life context. Case study research means single and multiple case studies, can include quantitative evidence, relies on multiple sources of evidence and benefits from the prior development of theoretical propositions. The case studies should not be confused with qualitative research and they can be based on any mix of quantitative and qualitative evidence. Single-subject research provides the statistical framework for making inferences from quantitative case-study data. [9] This is also supported and well-formulated in (Lamnek, 2005): "The case study is a research approach, situated between concrete data taking techniques and methodological paradigms."

When selecting a case for a case study, researchers often use information-oriented sampling, as opposed to random sampling. This is because the typical or average case is often not the richest in information. Extreme or atypical cases reveal more information because they activate more basic mechanisms and more actors in the situation studied. In addition, from both an understanding-oriented and an action-oriented perspective, it is often more important to clarify the deeper causes behind a given problem and its consequences than to describe the symptoms of the problem and how frequently they occur. Random samples emphasizing representativeness will seldom be able to produce this kind of insight; it is more appropriate to select some few cases chosen for their validity.

Three types of information-oriented cases may be distinguished:

1. Extreme or deviant cases,
2. Critical cases, and
3. Paradigmatic cases.

The extreme case can be well-suited for getting a point across in an especially dramatic way, which often occurs for well-known case studies such as in Freud's 'Wolf-Man.'

A critical case can be defined as having strategic importance in relation to the general problem. For example, an occupational medicine clinic wanted to investigate whether people working with organic solvents suffered brain damage. Instead of choosing a representative sample among all those enterprises in the clinic's area that used organic solvents, the clinic strategically located, 'If it is valid for this case, it is valid for all (or many) cases.' In its negative form, the generalization would be, 'If it is not valid for this case, then it is not valid for any (or only few) cases.'

The case study is effective for generalizing using the type of test that Karl Popper called falsification, which forms part of critical reflexivity. Falsification is one of the most rigorous tests to which a scientific proposition can be subjected: if just one observation does not fit with the proposition it is considered not valid generally and must therefore be either revised or rejected. Popper himself used the now famous example of, "all swans are white," and proposed that just one observation of a single black swan would falsify this proposition and in this way have general significance and stimulate further investigations and theory-building. The case study is well suited for identifying "black swans" because of its in-depth approach: what appears to be "white" often turns out on closer examination to be "black."

5.1.1 Assumptions

1. Cases selected based on dimensions of a theory (pattern-matching) or on diversity on a dependent phenomenon (explanation-building).
2. No generalization to a population beyond cases similar to those studied.
3. Conclusions should be phrased in terms of model elimination, not model validation. Numerous alternative theories may be consistent with data gathered from a case

study.

4. Case study approaches have difficulty in terms of evaluation of low-probability causal paths in a model as any given case selected for study may fail to display such a path, even when it exists in the larger population of potential cases.

In this chapter, six cases studies are presented to depict the overall stressful situations of the executive and non-executive employees of NTPC organization. The opinions are collected on the basis of personal interaction held with the executives and non executives and the perception is also being observed by the researcher at the work environment. In all the six cases a few commanalities and distinctive opinion is observed by the researcher. But all the cases exhibit the stressors which indicate prevalence of stress in the organization under study.

5.2 Case One: Mr. Madhu

Mr. Madhu is the senior manager aged about 52 years working in the IT department of the NTPC organisation. He belongs to backward caste community. He has 3 children who are in engineering and pharmacy graduation level studies. His wife is housewife and his parents are staying with him. He is from Throvagunta village, Ongole Mandal and Prakasham District. His parents are illiterates. He is the only one in his family who is doing job and all his other family members depend on agriculture. He joined in NTPC organization in the year 1984 with diploma qualification and later he has finished his graduation with B. Tech in electrical and electronics engineering. He has 25 years of experience in the organization. His duty is to monitor the systems which can record the power generation trend every second wise. The engineers would monitor all the computers in 7 stages of power generation. The organization has 2600MW capacity of power generation. In each stage 1, 2 and 3 200MWs power generation is taking place and in other 4 stages 2000MWs i.e., in each stage 500MWs capacity of power generation is being produced.

Mr. Madhu has to coordinate with the engineers who work in all those seven stages. He feel that lot of stress is involved as every second all the monitors are to be monitored and coordinated with other engineers. He feels that sometimes lack of coordination among managers and the department due to poor work relations, the work is being disturbed which caused stress. Apart from maintaining of the systems in the power plant, he is also responsible for providing the systems to all the departments with internet facility. Because of his over work load he is not able to coordinate and work properly. He feel that though this much work is being done but still he is not given recognition in his work and still he get pressure from the management to maintain quality in the work. He is also not comfortable with the work culture which is being maintained by his colleagues in the organization and he states that the organization is not able to take stress overcoming strategies. The organization depends on the outside contractors for ensuring the functioning of the systems. Apart from the power plant, in all other departments of the organization, whenever the systems shutdown takes place they have to wait till the contractors come and render the services. Mr. Madhu states that the delay is taking place in giving services to the organization as management is not particular about contractors work.

Mr. Madhu also points that the performance appraisal system is another parameter to feel stress in the organization as the evaluation take place regularly. Because of the poor relations with the management, most of the times he was degraded though his performance is good. He added that incidentally he was denied for getting promotion because of poor relations with the boss. The overall view of Mr. Madhu is that the work relationships in the organization are not up to the mark and the organization is not able to take up stress overcoming strategies.

While the discussion was going on Mr. Madhu Krishna has expressed that stress is existing due to heavy work load as he is forced to work for 10 to 12 hours in the plant in all seven stages. The engineers who were working with the department have resigned for the job and joined with Reliance power generation station. Though other two engineers were deputed but they were not able to share the work as they do not have much experience in the field. He pointed out that the working relations in the organization are not cordial many a times pressure is there from the management to maintain the operational quality in the plants.

Mr. Madhu case reveals that organizational stress among employees which has ultimate impact on TQM at NTPC.

5.3 Case Two: Mr. Rajan

Mr. Rajan is an executive in the department M&CS of NTPC Ramagumdam organization. He is aged about 54 years. He is an Engineering graduate. He belongs to scheduled caste communities. He has 3 children among whom one is married and other two are in engineering graduation. His wife is housewife and his parents lives in the village Rangampet, Shadnagar mandal of Mahabubnagar district. He is from poor family and all the family members depend on him for financial assistance. He has to take care his parents. He has 30 years of experience with the organization. He works with the materials department and his job is to see that the material is supplied to the power plant regularly. Constant monitoring of machineries, repairs and installation of machines in power plant and work sheds is the job of Mr. Rajan. He has to work with non executives like mechanics. He states that because of lack of coordination between management and workers, many a times the workers are not able to concentrate on the job and monitoring the machineries and repairs. Because of over involvement of employee unions in all the aspects of organization the work is suffered. He states that he has headache, depression and stress all the times whenever he comes to the department as work pressure is existing more. The organization is lacking close supervision of the activities.

He added that the management is not considering the opinion of the employees in taking the decisions.

Since the organization is the public sector unit, the workers are not particular about the functioning and performance. Because of the job security, the workers have negligible attitude towards organization and they never maintain work relations with the managers in the department. The workers point out that the job environment is not suitable as it involves lot of noise, dust, improper facilities in the work sheds. Mr. Rajan states that the issues have been brought to the notice of the management many times but still they have not responded well to these situations. Though organization focuses on performance all the times but it is not able to identify the needs of employees and promote the employees to the higher levels on time. He says that the job involves lot of stress as every movement repairs and installation of machineries will take place in the plant. The work used to get suffer due to damage of the machinery and it is the duty of the M & Cs department to look after all such things. Mr. Rajan is expressing his stress as the non executives never maintain punctuality and most of the times they argue with the department heads. Their job is routine and the promotion system for them is not the encouraging and due to this they never feel committed in working for the organization.

He pointed that he has overwork load as supplying of machineries and monitoring them is the constant problem. Though he is working for one shift but even during the other shifts also he has to share the work burden which is creating stress to him. Mr. Rajan is a skilled engineer and works with commitment in the organization. He says that he is attending to the emergency situations even during the night shifts when the problem arises but his colleagues are not able to accompany him when they are requested. He narrated the attitude of the management that that whenever he informs the management to consider his problems and assign the work to the other people, they were not able to accommodate him. He also expressed his discontentment regarding the promotion policy of the organization as he is not promoted to the higher position because of his community distinction.

Mr. Rajan's case exhibits higher workload assigned to the engineer, sudden calls for attending to repairs in different shifts, lack of timely promotions, caste and regional discriminations and bias of higher officials are the major stressors to executives at NTPC. There is an imperative need for the top management and officials to address these problems to improve organizational efficiency.

5.4 Case Three: Mr. John

Mr. John's is the senior manager in the HRD Department. He is aged about 56years. He has two children who have completed their graduation with engineering background and one is preparing for civil services and other one is trying for jobs. His parents are well educated and retired from government service as teachers. He hails from Rajamundry and belongs to scheduled caste community. He has MBA qualification along with his engineering degree. He has 28 years of work experience in the organization. He is working at Ramagundam plant since 8 years prior to this he worked in Utter Pradesh state in the same NTPC organisation. After getting promotion as senior manager he was shifted to NTPC Ramagundam unit. His job in the organization is to take care the manpower in the organization. The NTPC organization has regular staff and also hires workers from outside when ever work load is available. He states that most of the times he gets pressure from the employee unions in hiring the people. The HR policies of the organization are not suitable to the employees most of the times as they are not able to get promotions and other benefits. He states that sometimes the department heads do not consider the performance of employees in evaluating them and they give biased opinion based on region, religion, caste, community feeling. The managers also yield to the pressure of employee unions and try to promote the employees though they are not eligible or their performance is not up to the mark.

As far as promotion system to the executives is concerned, they may be transferred to the other plants without prior information even. This has caused great depression to the executives to move from one state to the other state to work in the same NTPC organization. In some situations even the non executives will also be transferred but it is within the organization only. Generally the non executives do not prefer to work in other departments because of new work environment. When the HR department takes such decision to transfer them they go for hesitation and employee unions involves in the situation. They do not focus on work and maintain the time. He gets pressure whenever the disciplinary action is being taken on employees. The major problem for the department is to allocate the manpower in plant during the shifts and allotting the work to the employees during the night shift has become constant problem. He adds that making manpower arrangement in the plant is another difficult task during the summer season. As the job environment involves lot of noise and dust. This has caused physical disorder to the employees most of the times like dehydration, allergy, breathing problems and headache. He opines that since close supervision in all the departments is not possible which is causing for decline in the performance and poor work relations. Providing the facilities in all the departments, focusing on the welfare measures to the employees has become difficult task to the department. He added that most of the times industrial accidents are taking place and immediately the department has to respond to the situation and take care of the employees. He says that his job has become too difficult to watch all the departments every time and attend immediately whenever the problem arises.

He says that he is the victim as he was not given the position as Deputy General Manager as his contemporaries have been promoted. When enquired the reason for not getting promotion as DGM he said that just because of the community back ground he was not given. He says that still suppressing the weaker sections of the society is taking place in the organization. He expressed that most of the times this kind of community feeling distinction is creating lot of stress and being frustrated.

Mr. John's case denotes his dissatisfaction in regard to promotion policy of NTPC. He observed a few flaws in performance evaluation of employees. The biased treatment of top officials, frequent and sudden transfers are important causes of stress among executives as per John's version.

5.5 Case Four: Mr. Shareef

Mr. Shreef's the diploma holder in architecture and working with technical services department in NTPC organization. He is aged about 56 years and he has 6 children. He has married two of his daughters and other four children are in studies with graduation and intermediate. He is from Venkatrao Palli village, Kodurupaka Mandal and Karimnagar District. He is the only one from his entire family who could acquire ITI certificate and doing job in the NTPC organization. He has completed his polytechnic diploma with mechanical engineering. His parents stay with him in the NTPC quarters. He stated that family responsibilities are creating lot of stress one side and the other side pressure from management to attend the problems whenever they arise in the NTPC plants.

He has 25 years of experience in the organization. His job is to monitor the machineries in the power plant. In the process of power generation, where ever repairs take place, he is suppose to attend and monitor them immediately. He opines that working with technical services department is difficult thing as they have to work in emergency situations. Whenever the problem arises with the machineries it is the duty of the technical services department to attend immediately. This involves lot of stress. He states in all the 7 stages of power generation, every day many problems are being raised and they are attending and providing technical services. This involves too much pressure and over work load. Sometimes due to power trip the technical services department has to rectify the problem immediately and see that the obstacle is not taking place in the power generation.

He opines that though technical services are provided whenever the need arises but still the management is not able to recognize the services and promote them to the higher levels. He says that promotion in executives is fast and effective but in case of non executives it is not the same. Neither the promotion system nor promotional avenues are good to the non-executives. The major problem in the organization is that management does not maintain good relations with the employees. Most of the times the workers who works with materials department, sheds and in plant got physical and psychological problem. The respondent quoted "Nelson Mandela was kept in prison till his strength is exhausted–we are also being treated in the same manner, the management is not promoting us to the higher position and they want to see that our strength is exhausted in the same position only".

Mr. Shareef stated that the non executives are not given opportunity to involve in the functioning of the organizational clubs or forums like welfare forums, sports clubs, plant councils, shop councils, workers education forums, training programmes also. He also adds that the work relations and management and employee relations are not up to the expected level and everywhere the non executives are suppressed and they were not given due recognition. In organization, the contractors involves more in day to day functioning of the organization as they have to supply the material to the departments. They do not supply on time and when they complain to the management, they do not respond immediately. The quality in tools also does not exist.

In case of training programmes, tours like national and international also, they executives get more opportunity rather than non-executives. Although technical knowledge is needed for the workers yet workers are not considered for availing such an opportunity. This also creates lot of stress as expressed by Shareef. During the informal discussion was held with Azeem, his overall view on management is that he is not happy with the relations maintained by the superiors in the organization as officials are subjective rather than objective in their approach. Mr. Shareef maintains that the non executives are not much involved in the welfare forums, sports councils, worker education forums. This pains the non-executives, resulting in strained relations between executives and non executives which ultimately scuttles TQM.

5.6 Case Five: Mr. Narain

Mr. Narain is a diploma holder working with the materials department. He hails from Anantharam village, Illanthakunta Mandal and Karimnagar District. He belongs to backward caste community. His wife is a housewife and he has 3 children. His children are in graduation and intermediate level. His parents lives in the village and he supports them financially and his sisters also. He joined in the service in 1985 after completion of ITI course. He has 24 years of experience in the organization and his qualification is diploma in mechanical engineering. He is working at the stage 1 plant. The stage 1, 2, and 3 are Italy technology based power generation plants and running with old technology and many a times power trip takes place in these plants and he should monitor the machineries and repair the engines whenever the problem arises. They are working in noisy environment which is creating stress and causing health problem. He says that the movement they enter into plant till they come out sound pollution is causing more stress. When ever more power generation is needed, these three plants would get lot of trouble. He told that their work is more stressful work in all three shifts of power generation. He states that management is not providing the needed facilities and they have to go with the minimum facilities which are existing in the plants. He also says that the discrimination between executives and non-executives is existing more in providing the facilities.

He expressed that most of the times they are getting pressure from the management to focus on constant power generation without any hurdle. Particularly working in the plant during summer season is another great problem due to hot. Health is being degraded and causing long term deceases. He is suffering from diabetes because of the work place stress. He states that when he was working in the plant particularly where coal is burned lot of noise and sound pollution is existing which has degraded the health standards. There were many occasions where he was hospitalized due to the work environment. Organization also does not care the employees and distribute work properly. Though this was brought to the notice of employee unions but still they were not able to do justice to overcome this kind of problem.

He narrated that because he has got lot of family responsibilities, whatever the salary that he is getting is not sufficient for him to care his family members. He says that financially he is struggling a lot and depending upon the hand loans most of the times. He narrated that he is having pressure from department head all the times that he gives importance to the Andhra region people as he belong to the same region and he suppress me most as I belong to Tenangana region. He pointed out that in the organization this kind of regional feelings are suppressing us and it is disturbing our family relations and work relations.

He says that as far as promotion part is concerned, still he is not satisfied with the good position for which he is eligible. He says that he has become victim because of the boss biased. There is adequate evidence that officials give importance to their own community and region people. It is very clear that the promotion policy of the organization is not properly designed. He opined that there are many problems but employees are adjusting with the situation as they pointed out that they do not have any other option to work. Finally, he concludes that most of the times because of the work place pressure and stress, the family life is also being affected.

Mr. Narain regards noise and sound pollution, working during summer in plant, lack of employee case, improper distribution of work, regional feeling and discrimination of officials as a few important stressors. Owing to stress and strain Mr. Narain is suffering from diabetes and other health problems. This micro level study of Mr. Narain supports the findings of the main study.

5.7 Case Six: Mr. Dinesh

Mr. Dinesh diploma is holder in electrical and electronics working with IT department in the organization. He aged about 42 years. He has 3 children. His wife is a housewife. He is from Ramakrishnapur village, Mandamarri Mandal and Adilabad District. His parents primarily depend on agriculture. They have 2 acres of land and with that the family used to survive. He joined in the NTPC organization in the year 1995. He has 15 years of experience in the organization. His main job is to see that all the departments are connected with Local Area Network. This helps the organization to monitor all the departments regularly. Since the organization is having 1600 employees with various departments, lot of work is involved in providing network to all these departments. There are only few employees in the IT department. Mr. Dayaker states that his job is involved with lot of stress as all the departments are to be connected through LAN. Failure of connection, problem with hardware and software of the systems are being attended by him. He says that he is attending the work on emergency basis with the assistance of his colleagues in the department. But another problem is poor work relations and lack of coordination between IT department and other departments.

He says that he is getting pressure from his manager to maintain the network. There are many systems which are being installed in each department. It is too difficult to monitor all these systems with few hands. The management is trying to get the services from the existing people only. Constant up gradation of the systems is the major problem to the department. Mr. Dayaker is not happy with the relations existing with the manager and other department. He says though he is working since 15 years but still he is not being promoted to the higher levels in the organization. He added that work recognition is not there in the organisation.

He expressed that no seniority or performance is considered in the promotion policy. The promotion system is depends on the opinion of the department head only. At the end of every financial year the performance of the employees is reviewed. After the end of the evaluation, the manager gives rating on the basis of four point scale opinion with the 4 options like–A. Poor, B. Good, C. Very good and D. Outstanding. Whoever gets outstanding for 4 years continuously, they would be promoted to the higher position. Most of the times the heads of the departments give biased opinion and they try to promote their own candidates based on the community, religion and region. This is frustrating the sincere workers and creating lot of stress. He adds that most of the times bossism is pinching the employees and with this poor work relations are existing in the organization. Sometimes they are experiencing the sleepless nights even because of relations at office and organizational policies are affecting the career of the employees.

He stated that the organization is not giving the employees the opportunity to be trained with latest software and hardware developments. This is also creating frustration in the organization as he has to update all the systems and provided needed network. He says that neither management nor employee unions are not in a position to take seriously about these problems. The employees are forced to adjust with the organization system and leading stressful life.

Mr. Dinesh's case depicts that information technology related stress of over workload, lack of proper inter and intra departmental coordination in NTPC. He complains that many a time no well defined promotion policy is followed and performance evaluation rating given by officials or boss plays a prominent role in the promotion of non-executives. He observed that non executives are at the mercy of the departmental head or manager and they are in a helpless position and lead stressful life.

All these cases reveal the typical stressors from the perception of executives and non executives of NTPC, Ramagundam unit. By and large these cases substantiate the elements or causes of employee stress reflected in the main study. The top management of NTPC and other officials concerned should address stressors denoted by the both levels executives and non executives to achieve the ultimate goal of TQM. This will ensure improvement in operational efficiency of the organization.

The next chapter deals with the summary of the thesis based on the observations during the study. It concludes the various issues covered for the research study. A few suggestions are also being made to the organization for better improvement of working relations and Total Quality Management.

5.8 Conclusion

Organizational stress has become a crucial factor for contemporary industrial organizations. It has gained significance as individual stress when accumulated, affects organizational efficiency. Many a times individual stress, if unchecked makes the organization dysfunctional. Fast changing economic environment, science and technology have turned the phenomenon of organizational stress more complex and complicated. Managing individual and organization has become a major challenge to the top management of both public and private sector enterprises. Organizational stress has become a universal problem to developing and developed economies. As it is related to individual and group of human factor, it has attracted the attention of experts and human resource management and the researchers.

Stress is part of everyday life for human factor. Stress refers to the demands, pressures or forces applied to human resources in an organisation. Stress also involves perception of threat about internal or external events. Threat stimulates the release of stress hormones which produce the 'fight-flight' response. The fight-flight response leads to physical, emotional and mental action which is essential for survival of employees in an organization. Initiatives like The Learning Organisation, Process Re-engineering, Diversity Training, Collaborative Team Work, and The High Performance Organisations are all affected by the way people perceive and respond to stress. The nature and environment of work is changing at greater pace. Perhaps now more than ever before, job stress posses a critical threat to the health of workers and in turn, to the health of organization.

When employees face the stressors a psychological imbalance takes place as a result of which fight-flight hormones are still activated. As an employee does not respond physically to these stressors, the hormones remain in human bodies leading to ongoing feelings of tension and anxiety. Positive management of stress results in positive emotions such as enjoyment, satisfaction, enthusiasm and excitement. However, too much stress can be debilitating when it causes detrimental changes in how one thinks, feels and behaves.

Stress has been a much and widely talked about phenomenon in the industrial world. It has featured in the Indian industrial organisations since 80's when the Indian market turned competitive. By now stress has become a major buzzword and legitimate concern of the times because it causes harm to both employees and organisations. To quote, a recent estimate is that stress is costing corporate America a staggering US$ 68 billion annually in lost productivity due to absences from work and stress claims costing up to 10 percent of company's earnings. It further reports that up to 90 percent of patients complain of stress-related symptoms and disorders. What is true of corporate America is true of corporate India also. Corporate employees stress has become a crucial factor in the recent past.

Work-related stress is a pattern of physiological, emotional, cognitive and behavioural reactions to some extremely taxing aspects of work content, work organization and work environment. When people experience work-related stress, they often feel tense and distressed and feel they cannot cope. Due to globalisation and changes in the nature of work, people in developing countries have to deal with increasing work-related stress. In industrialized countries people are becoming more familiar with what work-related stress is and how to manage it, however, in developing countries, this may not yet be the case. Although a few studies have been conducted in developing countries, particularly in Latin America, there are still not enough in-depth studies to fully analyse both cultural differences and behaviours which vary from one country to another. Along with existing difficulties in controlling other more well-known occupational risks, there is a lack of awareness of work-related stress, and shortage of resources to deal with it.

Stress is often understood in its negative expression as synonymous with distress. This is also how the concept of stress will be used in this report. However, it is worth bearing in mind that adapting to a new situation, even when the situation at first may be considered a threat, cannot entirely be seen as a negative process as overcoming the threat may be considered beneficial to personal growth and learning. As far as stress symptoms are concerned, a useful distinction can be made between short-term behavioural outcomes/maladaptive coping strategies, e.g. taking a sleeping pill, lighting up a cigarette, skipping breakfast, having an extra drink, and the more long-term consequences such as physical and mental ill health.

There is adequate empirical evidence which denotes a

correlation between organizational stress and total quality management. There seems an imperative need for modern organizations to manage stress and improve the performance of individual employees and the organization. Further stress results in decline in performance and it has an adverse impact on organization TQM. Stress is inevitable in human and organizational life, the management cannot be a silent spectator in regard to this phenomenon. The goal and objective of TQM cannot be achieved if the problem of an individual and the consequent organizational stress is not addressed properly.

5.9 Suggestions

The study shows that stress compromises a person's intellectual, emotional and interpersonal functioning. Literally every aspect of employee performance is hindered by stress. Organizational development, occupational health, employee assistance and human resources professionals can provide tremendous value to their organization by helping them effectively address this problem. The following suggestions are offered to address the problem of stress at NTPC to focus on total quality management.

5.9.1 Educate Decision-makers about the Human Capital: This is the most important step. Unless decision makers are cognizant of how stress affects their employees and their bottom line. During the research, it is observed that the relations between the heads of the department and the employees are not up to the mark. The decision makers of the departments need to give recognition to the efforts of their subordinates and reward them accordingly.

5.9.2 Help the Employees through Counselling: Every employee in the organization feel stress to some extent. They may be organizational or personal stressors. In order to overcome the stress, there is a need to have counselling and mentoring programmes which would give good results to achieve goals and more performance.

5.9.3 Identify the Stress Factors and Address them: The organization need to identify the key stress factors which causes in decline of performance. When organization recognizes the efforts of employees and rewards them with promotion and other privileges the performance would increase. As observed during the study, the key factors for the stress are poor work relations and improper promotion system. The non executives experience and calibre is to be considered in giving promotion. The organization norms are not to be changed in yielding to the pressure in any form. His may sound heretical, but the more confident employees are about their career options and marketability, the less time and energy will be diverted to worrying about their future. If they feel confident of their marketability, they can focus their attention on doing a good job, not on what they will do if they lose their job.

5.9.4 Involve Non-executives in Professional Forums: NTPC needs to consider non-executives in professional forums which results in greater job satisfaction as well as develops cordial relations in the organization.

5.9.5 Help Inter-personal Skills to both Management and Frontline Workers: Since much of the stress in the workplace is interpersonally generated, helping people improve in this area will reduce a significant source of emotional feelings.

5.9.6 Organise Change Management Training for all Employees: Since the rapid rate of change is rated as the top stressor for people, helping people at all levels in dealing with change will minimize the stress level throughout the organization. When the training programmes are conducted in the organization, the opportunity for the non-executives needs to be given priority. This will help in maintaining good relationship with the executives.

5.9.7 Protect the Interest of the Employees: This can be the focal point for any organization. As long as the interest of employees is protected, they would be motivated to put their hearts into the job. The protection of interests is with mutual consent and trust. Always the work place should be stress free environment.

Notes

1. Shepard, Jon; Robert W. Greene (2003). *Sociology and You.* Ohio: Glencoe McGraw-Hill. pp. A-22.
2. Robert K. Yin. *Case Study Research. Design and Methods.* Third Edition. Applied social research method series Volume 5. Sage Publications. California, 2002.
3. Bent Flyvbjerg, "Five Misunderstandings About Case Study Research." *Qualitative Inquiry*, Vol. 12, No. 2, April 2006, pp. 219-245.
4. Michel Crozier considers the case method as a clinical approach which is a study of particular cases to draw generalizations form the intimate understanding of theses. See Michel Crozier, The Bureaucratic Phenomenon, Chicago, the University of Chicago Press, 1964, pp. 4-5.
5. H. Odum – An Introduction to Social Research, p. 229.
6. Bargess Research Methods in Sociology, p. 26 in George Gurvitch and W.E Moore (eds.)Twentieth Century Sociology.
7. Pauline V. Young–Scientific Social Surveys and Research, p. 247.
8. Goode, William J. and Hatt, Paul K.–Methods of Social Research, 1952, p. 332.
9. Siegfried Lamnek. *Qualitative Sozialforschung*. Lehrbuch. 4. Auflage. Beltz Verlag. Weihnhein, Basel, 2005.

Appendix

Appendix

TQM at National Thermal Power Corporation (NTPC)

Efficiency in public enterprises is an important aspect of the studies in industrial as well as in managerial economics. It is the efficiency which determines the growth of a firm or an industry. The efficiency operated enterprise help to accelerate the rate of growth of an economy. But efficiency evaluation is a complex and multifaceted problem particularly in a public sector enterprise. Unlike in a private enterprise where the volume of profit earned is generally considered a reliable index of efficiency, the performance evaluation of a public enterprise is difficult proposition. The public enterprise is generally governed by the motto of serving the national interest, it has to meet several subjective criteria of excellence. But the question is how to judge the efficiency and the subjective performance of public sector enterprise.

In an economy like India where public sector enterprises have an important role to play, the evaluation of working of public enterprises is very essential. It is argued that the economy of the country is not properly growing due to the reason that public sector is not running efficiently. The low efficiency of public sector enterprises is the reason of low rate of development of industrial sector of the economy. This is the reason why in the new economic policy, the public enterprise's role in the economy has been curtailed and disinvestments policy has been adopted in the case of efficiently run public enterprise units of the country. The selected unit for the study NTPC is known for its quality in power generation and excellence in performance as well as profits. The economists have used a number of indices to judge the efficiency of public enterprises viz., net income, production, boost in sales, and factors of productivity and growth of the firm. But profit and profitability i.e., profitability on capital and profitability on sale are the most accepted criteria to judge efficiency of public as well as private enterprises.

The present study is conducted in National Thermal Power Corporation as it is one of the Nava Ratnas of Indian public sector units. NTPC is a leading public sector unit in generating power with different functionaries. This organisation has been awarded most of the times for maintaining its quality. The organisation has been giving much importance for performance which involves stress too. The study aims find out the relation between stress and total quality management. In order to achieve TQM, NTPC maintaining quality circles and professional circles. The employees have been divided into different groups and they were given authority and responsibility to maintain quality.

Profile of NTPC

Energy is an important parameter in the overall economic development activity of any Country. It has become synonymous with the progress in all fields of activities. Its standard of living in the words of Dagli is as follows "the difference between a starving Indian peasant and a prosperous American farmer is that behind his elbow the Indian farmer has almost nothing while his American counterpart has thousands of horse power. Thus, it is energy, which is the dividing line between any subsistence economy and a highly developed economy. India is poor and America is rich because America consumes nearly 50 times as much energy as is consumed by India. Energy is at the heart of the modern industrial society. It could also be an effective weapon in the battle against object poverty".

There is a close correlation between energy consumption and level of economic development. Energy means "capacity of doing work". There are various sources of energy but in India the important sources are coal, hydroelectricity, oil and natural gas, nuclear fuels, firewood and animal wastes. Despite the development of various sources in the energy sector, the fact still remains that low cast energy sources like fire wood, cattle dung and vegetable wastes account for as much as 45 percent of energy consumption in the country. Power development in India began in 1897 when a 200 kW hydro station was first commissioned at Darjeeling. In 1899, a first steam station was set-up in Calcutta with a total capacity of 100 kW.

Thereafter, a series of hydro and steam as is throughout the country in the most efficient and economic way, the state electricity board (SEBs) was constituted in the various states of the country under the provisions of the electricity (supply) act 1948. These SEBs, were to enjoy the monopoly in respect of generation, transmission and distribution of electricity in the country. After constitution of SEBs, there was phenomenal improvement in the development of installed capacity and power generation. The efficiency of working of power plant and their maintenance have been unsatisfactory as a result of which the power generating capacity already created could not have been fully utilized.

Power is the single factor, which changed the way of living. The National Thermal Power Corporation Limited, established on November 7, 1975, has become the most important infrastructure input for improving the standard of living to meet the growing demand and to fulfil the needs of the country. Just in 29 years this company has grown to be the largest producer of power in the country. NTPC is today India's largest power utility with an installed capacity of 24249 MW. Lighting up one fourth of the country through its 13 coal based, 7 gas based and 3 joint venture projects, NTPC plans to become a 66,000 MW company by the year 2017 in all over India.

NTPC is ranked sixth largest in then Asian pacific region and twenty fifth largest in the Asian pacific region and twenty fifth larger one in the world. As per the survey based on 1998 data carried out by data monitor UK, NTPC is the 6th largest in term of thermal generation and the second most efficient in terms of capacity utilization amongst top 10 utilities in the world. Today, NTPC has eleven cal and sin phased projects situated in various part of the country. This accounts for one fifth of the total generating capacity in the country. NTPC Ramagundam unit established with a approved capacity of 260MW and the present installed capacity is 2600MW which is the largest Thermal Power plant powering in India's growth. NTPC, Ramagundam unit credited with first ISO 14001 certified Super Thermal Power Station in our country.

NTPC a front-runner in the Indian Power Sector is one of the largest and the best power utilities of the world, there by contributing to India's emergence as one of the world's leading economies. The World Bank, in its performance audit report on NTPC's projects observed that, NTPC record in plant construction, cost containment and operating efficiency has been exceptional, while as an institution it has broken new ground in the organization and management, successfully navigated the transition from constructions to operating company and generally coped quite well with the problems of rapid expansion. Two corporations The National Hydro Electric Power Corporation (NHPC) and National thermal Power Corporation (NTPC) were set in 1975-76 in the Centre sector as a step to achieve the objectives. Keeping the significance of power supply in sight, NTPC has been chosen for the purpose of the study as it has many units under its control. Ramagundam Super Thermal Power Station (RSTPS) has been selected for the study.

Objectives of NTPC

1. To add generating capacity within prescribed time and cost.
2. To operate and maintain power stations at high availability ensuring minimum cost of generation. It has planned massive growth to make itself a 66,000 MW company.

3. To maintain the financial soundness of the company by managing the financial operations in accordance with good commercial utility practices.
4. To function as a responsible corporate citizen and discharge social responsibility, in respect of environment protection and rehabilitation. The corporation will strive to utilize the ash produced at its stations to the maximum extent possible through production of ash bricks, building materials etc.
5. To adopt appropriate human resources development policy leading to creation of team of motivated and competent power professionals. To introduce, assimilate and attain self-sufficiency in technology, acquire expertise in utility management practices. And to disseminate knowledge essentially as a contribution to other constituents of the power sector in the country.
6. To develop research and development for achieving improved plant reliability.
7. To expand the consultancy operations and to participate in ventures abroad.

NTPC Vision

"A world class integrated power major, powering India's growth, with increasing global presence".

Corporate Core Values (BCOMIT):

- Business Ethics.
- Customer Focus.
- Organizational and Professional Pride.
- Mutual Respect and Trust.
- Innovation and Speed.
- Total Quality for excellence.

NTPC Mission:

- Make available reliable and quality power in increasingly large quantities at appropriate tariffs, and ensure timely realization of revenues
- Speedily plan and implement power projects, with

contemporary technology.

NTPC Power Projects:

NTPC has 13 coal based super thermal power projects at Singrauli, Korba, Ramagundam, Karaka, Kahalgoan, Dadri, Vindhyachal, Rihand, Telcher Kaniha, Unchaher, and Talcher TPS, out of the these Singrauli, Korba and Ramagundam have achieved their approved capacity. NTPC has 7 gas-based power stations.

NTPC Organization and Functions

The organization design is one of the main factors, which ultimately determines the effectiveness of an enterprise. The board of directors is the supreme policy making body, which give the direction to the activities of the organization. The head of this board is the chairman and managing director who is also the full time chief executive of the company. The members of this board are both full-time directors as well as senior level officers.

The basic divisions, which are accountable to CMD, are:

1. Technical and engineering division.
2. Corporate Commercial division.
3. Operation Services division.
4. Corporate Finance division.
5. Corporate Human Resources division.
6. Corporate Projects division.
7. Vigilance division.

Initiatives

NTPC Electricity Supply Company Ltd. has been formed to take up power distribution activities. NTPC Vidyut Vyapar Nigam has been formed as a subsidiary company for power trading. The excess power available with NTPC during the off-peak periods will be sold by this company. NTPC Hydro Ltd., incorporated as a subsidiary company to take up similar hydro projects. The Company is also planning to enter the coal mining and coal washeries business.

Ramagundam Super Thermal Power Station Profile

Ramagundam, the sage of a Super Thermal power station was built along the southern banks of the river Godavari in Karimnagar Dist. of Andhra Pradesh. NTPC, Ramagundam was the 3rd in the series of thermal power station set by the organization. The foundation stone was laid on 14.11.1978 by late Sri Morarji Desai, the Prime Minister of India.

According to the mythological legend lord Rama visited Ramagundam during the exile period. His holy feet are enshrined in a monument which has been preserved over the centuries.

Mission

1. Make available reliable and quality power in increasingly large quantities tariffs and ensure timely realization of revenues.
2. Promote consultancy and make prudent acquisitions.
3. Speedily plan and implement power projects with contemporary technology.
4. Continuously develop competent human resources to match world standards.

Vision

To be one of the world's largest and best power utilities, powering India's growth".

Environment Management

1. The station was accredited with ISO-14001EMS by M/s Loyds Register Quality Assurance, U.K. for Environmental Management.
2. LWTP to conserve water
3. Ash utilization.
4. Environmental studies to upgrade environmental quality.
5. To ensure complains to statutory requirements.
6. Review and update disaster management.
7. Systematic monitoring effluents, stack emission and

ambient air.

RSPTS Organization and Functions

The projects Organization leaded by general manager is interested with the total responsibility for implementation of all aspects of the projects in according with the master. Network schedule and the operation and the maintenance of the running units in a most cost effective manner; refer chart-11 for functional organization of RSTPS. The same have been explained below.

Project Organisation: These two basic executing functions under this are 'civil construction" and 'equipment erection". The "civil construction" takes care of all the civil activities from survey and soil investigation site leaving infrastructure development township construction etc.

Operation and Maintenance: This development looks after the operation of commission units and the shorts, long term maintenance, works; O&M includes main plants operation, mechanical maintenance, electrical maintenance, control and instrumentation maintenance, fuel handling (O&M), chemistry and coal Transportation (MGR) groups.

Materials Management: This group under takes the control of bulk structure construction materials like steel, Cement, diesel and fuel oil apart from procurements storage and control of consumables, equipment and spare parts.

Personnel Administration: The development looks after the recruitment and establishment along with training of the Site personnel and the industrial relation and welfare activities of the project and also generates Administration and township organization and other miscellaneous activities.

Planning and System: This group used to provide constant information regarding the progress of every single projects activity.

Field Quality Surveillance: This group supplements the efforts of constructional erection engineers in meeting the Norms of quality by providing specialized as well as by conducting advanced tests.

Finance and Accounts: This deportment has been entrusted with the responsibilities of processing work finance and material finance cases. This function also carries out audit, maintenance of accounts and stock verification activities

Objectives of the Study

The primary objective of the study is to examine employee stress in NTPC organisation and its impact on Total Quality Management. The following are the other objectives of the study.

1. To identify the stressors in the organisation which affect the performance of employees'.
2. To know the nature and extent of correlation between stressor and performance.
3. To examine the role of professional and quality circles in maintaining total quality management.
4. To evaluate the impact of stress on total quality management.
5. To identify the problems related to TQM at unit under study.

Hypothesis

1. Work-related stress is a health and safety issue as well as an important factor for Total Quality Management.
2. Work-related stress can be managed within the same logical and systematic way as other health and safety issues.
3. The management of stress at work is based on the adaptation and application of a control cycle approach such as that made explicit in contemporary models of risk management.

The main focus of the research work implies the impact of stress on TQM. First, there is a rich of scientific data on work stress, its causes and effects, and on some of the mechanisms underpinning the relationships among these like stress and performance which leads to total quality management. What is required is an answer to the outstanding methodological questions, and to more specific questions about particular aspects of the overall stress process and its underpinning mechanisms.

Second, although this wealth of scientific data exists, it still needs to be translated into practice, and the effectiveness of this practice evaluated. This is another set of needs, and one that will only be settled outside the laboratory and through the development of consensus and eventually common practice. While stress at work remains a major challenge to occupational health. The present research work assumes.

Methodology

The present study intends to examine the impact of employee stress on TQM. For the purpose of the study NTPC, Ramagundam unit operating at Karimnagar district is selected. This study is based on both the primary and secondary data. Primary data is collected from executives and non executives working at NTPC. For the purpose of investigation a sample of 90 respondents is drawn from the category of executives and 180 from the category of non executives. A sample is selected on the basis of purposive random sampling method. A structured questionnaire was administered to both the executives and non executives of employees. The sample consists of 6.4 percent of executives and 6.2 percent of non executives. The study was conducted during 2005-2008. The NTPC unit was selected because of its reputation in adopting TQM concept and policy as for its outstanding performance as one of the Navaratnas among existing public sector organizations in the country.

Size of Sample

For the purpose of conducting research the sample size is being selected 90 employees out of 580 executives and 180 employees out of 1126 non executives. There are around 1706 employees are working in the organisation with different positions.

Table A1: Sample Size for the Research Work at NTPC Ramagundam Unit

S.N	Type of Employees	Total Number	Sample Number
1.	Executives	580	90
2.	Non-executives	1126	180
	Total	1706	270

Limitations of the Study

1. NTPC Ramagundam unit has been selected for the purpose of the study both as per consideration of dearness of the researcher rather than any scientific base.
2. A too narrow view has been taken of what constitutes employee stress and its management.
3. One concept of stress has weak theoretical base and based on subjective thinking of individuals.
4. It is assumed that employee organizational stress (stress at work place) has adverse impact on TQM.
5. Stress management strategy adopted by NTPC focuses on single type of intervention and very rarely multiple strategies are offered. Hence, the impact of stress on TQM is studied with focus on single type of intervention.
6. The impact of stress on TQM is studied on the bases of response/reaction of respondents comprising sample from executives and non executives. This method has its own deficiency.

Period of Study

The research study is undertaken from December 2005 to November 2008. During the study schedules have been administered to the respondents and collected their response. Observation method is also adopted during the study to get the needed information for making conclusion that stress will have impact on total quality management in NTPC organization.

TQM at NTPC Ramagundam

While NTPC continues to perform well, rapid changes in the business environment have necessitated adoption of newer approaches in enhancing the overall competitiveness of the organisation. NTPC needs to develop a culture of continuous and breakthrough improvements to realize its vision of becoming a world class power utility. 'Total Quality' and 'Customer Focus' have been adopted as two of the significant core values, both being key elements of TQM.

TQM efforts in NTPC were brought to the fore in 1997-98 by launching the Quality Circles. From a humble beginning, soon the QC movement grew by leaps and bounds and engulfed the entire work force of supervisors and workmen. By April 2002, a total of 859 Quality Circles involving 7,124 QC members were in existence. A large number of executives also got involved in the QC movement by acting as QC facilitators, trainers and co-ordinators.

The success of this experiment encouraged NTPC to launch other TQM initiatives. '5S' and Benchmarking came next and were very well received by various Stations and Projects. 'Six Sigma' and 'Knowledge Management' are the emerging TQM initiatives to take shape in NTPC in the near future. To manage the whole gamut of TQM initiatives, NTPC has put in place a suitable organisation structure and adopted only a select few TQM tools in the first phase of its TQM journey.

With the success and gains of on going TQM initiatives, it had become increasingly important to give a formal structure to TQM processes. In August 2002, a new TQM Division was set up under a full time Executive Director. An apex level TQM Steering Council was constituted at corporate level having involvement of Directors and Executive Directors. With the creation of a separate TQM Division, systematic attempt to develop culture of continuous improvements in the company has just begun. We need to accelerate the movement by learning from experts and experience of other organizations.

To have a strong and empowered institutional set up in the organisation for TQM, an organisation structure has been sanctioned by CMD based on strong feed back and recommendations of EDs/GMs. The structure with role and responsibilities entrusted to TQM Groups set up at Corporate level, Regional level and Station/Project level.

Quality Circles at NTPC

Quality Circle is a small group of employees, roughly 6 to 8 in number, doing similar type of work, who voluntarily sit together at regular intervals to identify, analyze and create innovative solutions to work related problems. Quality Circles have had Origin in Japan, based on work done by Dr. Deming, Dr. Juran and Dr. Ishikawa. Quality Circles is an ideal intervention for Human Resource Development at the grass root levels. It establishes a close relationship between workers and productivity. Quality Circles aim at self-actualization of QC members. This is quite evident as the initiative enhances their team spirit, creativity, confidence and presentation skills. Quality Circles movement in NTPC was revived in the year 1997-98 when NTPC had only 78 circles with 624 members. Continuous encouragement provided at all levels of management has resulted in formation of more than 850 Quality Circles with around 12000 members till April, 2007 have been working in NTPC units in India. NTPC has targeted to achieve 80 percent membership of its workers and supervisors in the QC movement. Success of Quality Circles in NTPC can be attributed to implementing an effective support structure involving dedicated efforts of a large number of Facilitators and Coordinators.

Professional Circles at NTPC

This is an initiative introduced in the year 1997-98 to

provide freedom and space to executives to get together, network and share knowledge, learning and experience on issues of professional interest. Professional Circles are formed voluntarily in most of the plants. Roughly there are about 250 Professional Circles in NTPC. The participants of the Professional Circle meet once in a month and share professional information relating to their areas of work. The process of sharing is generally done through presentations made by some of the participants. The presentations made in the Professional Circles across the company are also collected at the regional level and recorded for reference. An Annual Professional Circle meet is organized at every project and station.

NTPC's Approach

NTPC has decided to apply CII's Business Excellence Model for getting comprehensive assessment about its performance. CII, TQM group has already made presentations showing the concept and a roadmap of long term Quality Improvement Plan through the Business Excellence Model. It is planned to introduce this model initially at Dadri. Through this, Dadri will get an outside perspective on its business processes based on a review by a team of external experts. Results of this review are distilled in a detailed feedback report, which will outline strengths, and opportunities for improvement based on the award criteria.

Feedback report can be used to energize and guide organizational improvement programs. CII's business excellence model consists of nine elements called "enablers" and "results", each totalling 500 points. In order to be eligible for detailed assessment by external experts, it is essential to score a minimum of 350 points out of 1000 on the basis of report to be submitted by Dadri.

Strategies Adopted to Overcome Stress

The focus of this report is on stress within a work context

at NTPC Ramagundam unit. However, we acknowledge that factors outside work, e.g. personal relationships and family circumstances, will influence and interact with stressful situations and vice versa. For example, a negative development in a person's domestic life, may make them more vulnerable to pressure in the workplace. In turn intolerable workloads over a long time period are likely to affect an individual's functioning at home, thereby possibly influencing their relationships with their spouse and children.

Stress is increasingly becoming accepted as a workplace phenomenon negatively affecting a growing number of people across the world. As the economy becomes global and competition increases in the battle for market shares and survival, pressure mounts on workers. With high levels of crime and aggression in society, violence finds its way into the workplace in the form of robbery and assaults, particularly on front-line staff and service providers. As pressures mount aggression may also build up within the workplace, making worker on worker violence more likely. Stress has become part and parcel of life. As long as organizations survive, to exist in the competition pressure should be there to the worker. When the pressure increases it leads to stress and downfall of performance also.

The economic world is moving towards a single, global market place. However, this economic globalisation has increased commercial competition with growing pressures on everyone at work as a result. In order to survive in this competitive environment, organisations are restructuring and downsizing with the aim of cutting costs. Tendering for contracts, which also now often include public services has become increasingly common, bringing with it more economic risk-taking in order to reduce cost. Organisational downsizing and restructuring has resulted in greater pressure on those remaining employees with an increase in workload and work pace. Such work-intensification has resulted in employees in some countries. In order to increase flexibility a growing number of people are being offered work on a temporary or part-time basis and sub-contracting or outsourcing has become common in many countries. Perceptions of job insecurity are also increasing in the industrialised world. Even though such perceptions at times may be at odds with reality, they reflect a trend affecting a number of people.

Stress Factors at NTPC Ramagundam Unit

Work Place Stress: It is observed during the research period at the plant and had informal interaction with the employees which denotes that stress is existing in the organisation. The executive and non executive employees when they are working in the plant, they have stress due to sound pollution, dust, hot condition, constant repairs of the machineries, trip of the units in generating the power are causing stress to both the category of employees. The power generation takes place during three shifts of NTPC organization and employees who work during night shifts feel more stress in comparison with other shifts.

Problems due to Poor Relationships: This is the another factor found during the research in the NTPC organization. It is observed that the work relations in the organization are not up to the mark. The biased opinion of officials in performance appraisal is causing poor relations. When the employees are not given promotion based on their performance and experience, they feel stress. In some situations, the sincere employees have become victims because of the promotion policy and biased evaluation of department head as expressed by the employees during the informal interaction. The regional feeling is another parameter to have poor relations in the organization.

Employee Dissatisfaction towards Management: This is due to lack of coordination and cooperation between management and employees. Whenever employees express their discontentment at the work place, the management has to take into consideration to resolve the issues of the employees.

In many a times the employees problems are not addressed properly as stated by the employees. The promotion system to the employees is not implemented properly. It is observed that many employees are in the same position for longer period due to delay in promotion. This causing more dissatisfaction to the employees in the organization.

Poor Commitment towards Work and Organisation: The micro level study conducted in the organization substantiates the main study that the commitment towards work and organization is lacking. It is observed that recently many executives have resigned for their service in the NTPC and joined with Reliance power generation centres. The non-executives performance in the organization is not up to the expectations of the management. NTPC organization is depending upon the daily wage labourers and contractual service employees. Due to lack of commitment towards organization, many a times the work is being disturbed. This indicates that stress is existing in the organization.

Focus by the Organization and TQM Evaluation: The organization is very particular in maintaining the quality in utilization of resources in generating the power. Many a times the NTPC Ramagundam unit has bagged awards at national and international level. The organization has TQM department which focuses on quality and professional circles to maintain the standards of the organisation. Apart from the regular job, the employees have to join in these forums to share the views regarding performance improvement. When organization is putting pressures to maintain the standards of the organization, causing stress to the employees as observed during the study period. The organization is very particular in evaluating the performance of the employees regularly. This certainly causes stress to the employees as they need to check their performance at regular intervals. All these factors indicate that stress is existing in the organisation.

The initiation regarding overcoming of stress is well taken by the organization. It is continuously conducting the training programmes to both the category of employees like executives and non executives. All the employees are given opportunity join in the forums to develop cordial relations at the work place and sometimes the informal meetings are also arranged to have socializing phenomenon.

Bibliography

Bibliography

A.D. Hart, The Hidden Link between Adrenalin & Stress 1991, p. 19.

Abel, T.M., Metraux, R., and Roll, S. (1987) Psychotherapy and Culture, University of New Mexico Press, Albunquerque.

Albrecht, K. 1979. Stress and the Manager. Englewood Cliffs, NJ: Prentice-Hall.

Allen, R.J. (1983). Human Stress: Its nature and Control. Minneapolis, MN: Burgess Publishing Company.

Andrews, F.M., & Farris, G.F. (1972). Time pressure and performance of scientists and engineers: A five-year panel study. Organizational Behaviour and Human Performance, 8, 185-200.

Argyris, C. (1990) Overcoming organizational defences, Needham Heights, MA, Allyn, Bacon.

Argyris, Chris (1991) Teaching Smart People How to Learn Harvard Business Review, 69, 3, 99-109.

Argyris, Chris (1994) Good Communication That Blocks Learning Harvard Business Review, 72, 74, 77- 85, July-August 1994.

Arno Steen Andreasen.(2003) How to deal with the stress of life through Logo therapy, pp.12-13.

Arnold, H.J., and Feldman. 1986. Organizational Behaviour. New York Lazarus, R.S., & Folkman, S.(1984). Stress, appraisal and coping. NewYork: Springer Publishing Co.

Arsenault, A., and S. Dolan, "The Role of Personality, Occupation, and Organization in Understanding the Relationship between Job Stress, Performance, and Absenteeism," Journal of Occupational Psychology, Vol. 56, 1983, pp. 227-240.

Asthana, H.S. (1983). The Concept of Stress: A Phenomenological Approach; Paper presented at the seminar on stress, anxiety and mental health, University of

Allahabad.

Attention," Quarterly Journal of Experimental Psychology, Vol. 29, No. 4, November 1977, pp. 651-667.

Bammer, K., & Newberry, B.H. (1983). Stress and Cancer. Toronto: C.J. Hogrefe.

Bargess Research Methods in Sociology, p. 26 in George Gurvitch and W.E Moore (eds.)Twentieth Century Sociology.

Barnett, R. (2000) Working Knowledge. In Garrick and Rhodes (2000) Research and Knowledge at Work: Perspective, Case studies and Innovative Strategies, London: Routledge.

Beehr, T.A., Jex, S.M., Stacy, B. A., & Murray, M.A. (2000). Work stressors and co-worker support as predictors of individual strain and job performance. Journal of Organizational Behaviour, 21, 391-405.

Beer, M. and Eisenstat, R.A. (2000) The silent killers of strategy implementation and learning, Sloan Management Review, 41, 4, 29-40.

Beer, M., Eisenstat, R.A. and Spector, B. (1990) Why change program do not produce change, Harvard Business Review, November-December, 1990.

Benson, Herbert 1985. Beyond the Relaxation Response. New York: Berkley Books.

Bent Flyvbjerg, "Five Misunderstandings About Case Study Research." Qualitative Inquiry, Vol. 12, No. 2, April 2006, pp. 219-245.

Bhagat, R. S. 1983. "Effects of stressful life events on individual performance effectiveness and work adjustment processes within organizational settings: A research model." Academy of Management Review. 8(4): 660-671.

Borman, W.C., & Motowidlo, S.J. (1993). Expanding the criterion domain to include elements of contextual performance. In N. Schmitt & W. Borman (Eds.), Personnel selection in organizations (pp. 71-98). New York: Jossey-Bass.

Bowers, C., J. Weaver, and B. Morgan, Jr., "Moderating the Performance Effects of Stress," in James Driskell and Eduardo Salas, eds., Stress and Human Performance, Hillsdale, N.J.: Lawrence Erlbaum Associates, 1996, pp. 163-192.

Bunce, D., & West, M. (1994). Changing work environments: innovative coping responses to occupational stress. Work and Stress, 8, 319-331.

Buzzell, R.D. and Gale, B.T. (1987) The PIMS Principles: Linking Strategy to Performance, New York, Free Press.

Campbell, J.P., McCloy, R.A., Oppler, S.H., & Sager, C.E. (1993). A theory of performance. In E. Schmitt, W.C. Borman, & Associates (Eds.), Personnel selection in organizations (pp. 35-70). San Francisco: Jossey-Bass.

Campbell, MAJ S., CPT D. Ritzer, SGT J. Valentine, and COL R. Gifford, Operation Joint Guard, Bosnia: An Assessment of Operational Stress and Adaptive Coping Mechanisms of Soldiers, Washington, D.C.: Walter Reed Institute of Research, 1998.

Cannon-Bowers, J., and E. Salas, "Individual and Team Decision-Making Under Stress: Theoretical Underpinnings," in J. Cannon-Bowers and E. Salas, eds., Making Decisions Under Stress, Washington, D.C.: American Psychological Association, 1998, pp. 17-37.

Childre, D., and Martin, H.(1999). The Heartmath Solution, San Francisco: Hyper San Francisco.

Clarke, T., Rollo, C. (2001) Corporate initiatives in knowledge management. Education +Training, p. 43.

Compaq (1999) Knowledge Management: Approaching Solutions. White Paper, Compaq Computer Corporation, Houston, TX.

Cox, T. & Griffiths, A.J. (1995) The assessment of psychosocial hazards at work. In M.J. Shabracq, J.A.M. Winnubst & CL Cooper (Eds.) Handbook of Work and Health Psychology. Chichester: Wiley & Sons.

Cox, T. (1978) Stress. Macmillan, London.

Cox, T. (1985a) The nature and measurement of stress. Ergonomics, 28, 1155-1163.

Cox, T. (1987). Stress, coping and problem solving. Work & Stress, 1, 5-14.

Cox, T. (1988a) Psychobiological factors in stress and health. In S. Fisher & J. Reason (eds.) Handbook of Life Stress, Cognition and Health. Wiley & Sons, Chichester.

Cox, T. (1990) The recognition and measurement of stress: conceptual and methodological issues. In: E. N. Corlett & J. Wilson (eds.) Evaluation of Human Work. Taylor & Francis, London.

Cox, T., & Cox, S. (1993) Psychosocial and Organizational Hazards: Monitoring and Control. Occasional Series in Occupational Health, No. 5. World Health Organization (Europe), Copenhagen, Denmark.

Cropanzano, R., D. Rapp, and Z. Byrne, "The Relationship of Emotional Exhaustion to Work Attitudes, Job Performance, and Organizational Citizenship Behaviours," Journal of Applied Psychology, Vol. 88, No. 1, February 2003, pp. 160-169.

Deming, Edwards, W. (1986), Out of the Crisis, Cambridge, Massachusetts Institute of Technology, Centre for Advanced Engineering Study.

Deming, W. Edwards (1982) Quality Productivity and Competitive Position Cambridge, Mass.: MIT, Centre for Advanced Engineering Study

Dewe, P. (1987) New Zealand ministers of religion: identifying sources of stress and coping strategies. Work & Stress, 1, 351-363.

Dewe, P. (1993) Work, stress and coping: common pathways for future research? Work & Stress, 7(1), 1-3.

Dewe, P. (2000) Measures of coping with stress at work: a review and critique. In P. Dewe, M. eiter & T. Cox (eds.) Coping, Health and Organisations. London: Taylor & Francis.

Dewe, P., Leiter, M & Cox, T (Eds.) (2000) Coping, Health

and Organisations. London: Taylor & Francis.

DiMaggio, P.J. and W.W. Powel (1983) "The iron cage revisited: Institutional

Baum, A. 1994. Behavioural, biological, and environmental interactions in disease process. In S. Blumenthal, K. Matthews, & S. Wiess (eds.).

C. Cooper and R. Pyne, Stress at Work; and S. Parasuraman and J.A. Alutto. Campion, A., Medsker, G. J. and Higgs, C., 'Relation between work group characteristics and effectiveness: Implications for designing an effective work group', in Personnel Psychology, Vol. 46, No. 4, 1993, pp. 823-850.

Compas, B.E., Banez, G.A., Malcarne, V., & Worsham, N.(1991). Perceived control and coping with stress: A developmental perspective. Journal of Social Issues, 47(4),2 3-34.

Cooper, C.L., & Marshall, J. (1976) Occupational sources of stress: a review of the literature relating to coronary heart disease and mental ill health. Journal of Occupational Psychology, 49, 11-28.

Cox, T. & Thomson, L. (2000) Organisational healthiness: work-related stress and employee health. In P. Dewe, M. Leiter & T. Cox (Eds.) Coping, Health and Organisations. London: Taylor & Francis.

Cox, T. (1993) Stress Research and Stress Management: Putting theory to work.

Doherty & Tyson, S. (1998) Mental Well-being in the workplace. H&SE.

Dohrenwend, B.S., & Dohrenwend, B.P. (1974) Stressful Life Events: Their Nature and Effects. Wiley & Sons, New York.

Dohrenwend, B. S., Krasnoff, L., Askenasy, A.R., and Dohrenwend, B. P. (1988) The Psychiatric Epidemiology Research Interview Life Events Scale. In: L. Goldberg & S. Breznitz (eds.) Handbook of Stress: Theoretical and Clinical Aspects. Free Press, New York.

Driskell, J., R. Carson, and P. Moskal, Stress and Human

Performance: Final Report, Orlando, Fla.: Naval Training Systems Centre, August 15, 1988.

Easterbrook, J. A., "The Effect of Emotion on Cue Utilization and Organization of Behaviour," Psychological Review, Vol. 66, 1959, pp. 183-201.

Edward A. Charlesworth & Ronald G. Nathan (1984) "The Distress and Wellness Cycle" from Stress Management, A Comprehensive guide to wellness

Einhorn, H.J., & Hogarth, R.M. (1981) Behavioural decision theory: processes of judgement and choice. Annual Review of Psychology, 32, 53-88.

Eraut, M., Alderton, J., Cole, G., Senker, P. (1998) Learning from Other People at Work. In Coffield, F (ed.), Learning at Work. Bristol: The Policy Press

Ernst and Young and American Quality Foundation (1992), The international quality study: The definitive study of the best international quality management practices: top-line findings, Ernest & Young, Cleveland, OH.

Everitt & Dunn (1991) and Polit (1996) provide more detail about the use and interpretation of Wilks' lambda. Further reading Everitt B.S. & Dunn G. (1991) Applied Multivariate Data Analysis. Edward Arnold. London. pp. 219-220.

Fay, D., & Sonnentag, S. (2001). Stressors and personal initiative: A study on organizational behaviour. Manuscript submitted for publication, Stress in Organizations.

Fisher, S. (1996) Life change, personal control and disease. South African Journal of Psychology, Vol. 26, No. 1, pp. 16-22.

Fletcher, B. C. (1988) The epidemiology of occupational stress. In: C.L. Cooper & R. Payne (eds.) Causes, Coping and Consequences of Stress at Work. Wiley & Sons, Chichester.

Folkman, S. (1984). Personal control and stress and coping processes: a theoretical analysis. Journal of Personality and Social Psychology, 46, 839-852.

French, W. L., Kast, F. E., and Rosenzweig, J. E. 1985.

Understanding Human Behaviour in Organizations. New York: Harper & Row.

Friedman, I. A., and L. Mann, "Coping Patterns in Adolescent Decision-Making: An Israeli-Australian Comparison," Journal of Adolescence, Vol. 16, 1993, pp. 187-199.

Friedman, M., & Rosenman, R.H. (1974). Type A Behaviour and Your Heart. Connecticut: A Fawcett Crest Book.

Friedman, M., and Rosenman, R. 1974. Type A Behaviour and Your Heart. New York: Knopf.

Furnham., A., Forde., L., and Ferrari., K. Personality and work motivation. Personality and Individual Differences (1999), Vol. 26(6), 1035-1043.

Gaillard, A.W.K., and F.J.M. Steyvers, "Sleep Loss and Sustained Performance," in A. Coblentz, ed., Vigilance and Performance in Automatized Systems, Dordrecht, The Netherlands: Kluwer Academic Publishers, 1989.

Goldberg, R.J. & Novack, D.H. (1992) The psychosocial review of systems. Social Science & Medicine, Vol. 35, No. 3, pp. 261- 269.

Goode, William J & Hatt, Paul K–Methods of Social Research, 1952, p. 332.

Goodheart, Annette (1994). Laughter Therapy. Santa Barbara. Less Stress Press.

Griffiths, A.J. (1999a) Work design and management-The older worker. Experimental Aging Research, 25 (4), pp.411-420.

H. Odum–An Introduction to Social Research, p. 229.

Hackman, J. R. and Wageman, R. (1995) Total quality management: Empirical, conceptual and practical issues. Administrative Science Quarterly, 40, 309-342.

Halverson, CPT R., CPT P. Bliese, SGT R. Moore, and CPT C. Castro, Psychological Well-Being and Physical Health Symptoms Deployed for Operation Uphold Democracy: A Summary of Human Dimensions Research in Haiti, Washington, D.C.: Walter Reed Army Institute for Research, 1995.

Hart, Arachibald D. (1991). The Hidden Link Between Adrenalin and Stress. Dallas: Word.

Hart, Archibald D. (1999). The Anxiety Cure. Nashville: Word.

Hatton, C., et al., "Stressors, Coping Strategies, and Stress Related outcomes Among Direct Care Staff in Staffed Houses for People with Learning Disabilities," Mental Handicap Research, Vol. 8, 1995, pp. 252-271.

Hayes, Treasa (1997) The Learning Organisation: Fashionable Fad or Path to Progress? www.globalresearchbusiness.com.

Hendricks, K. B. and Singhal, V. (1997) Does implementing an effective TQM program actually improve operating performance? Empirical evidence from firms that have won quality awards. management Science, 43, 1258-1274.

Hendricks, K. B. and Singhal, V. (2001) The long-run stock price performance of firms with effective TQM programs. Management Science, 47, 359-368.

Hockey, G. R. J. (2000). Work environments and performance. In N. Chmiel (Ed.), Work and organizational psychology: a European perspective (pp. 206-230). Oxford: Blackwell.

Hockey, G. R., Maule, A. J., Vlough, P. J., & Bdzola, L. (2000). Effects of negative mood states on risk in everyday decision making. Cognition and Emotion; 14, 823-856.

Holmes, T. H., & Rahe, R. H. (1967) The Social Readjustment Rating Scale. Journal of Psychosomatic Research, 11, 213-218.

Holmes, T. H., & Rahe, R. H. The Social Readjustment Rating Scale (1999). In the stress consultancy Stress Management Training. Shefield: The Stress Consultancy.

Holmes, T. H., & Rahe, R. H. The Social Readjustment Rating Scale (1999). In the stress consultancy Stress Management Training. Shefield: The Stress Consultancy.

Idzikowski, C., and A. D. Baddeley, "Fear and Dangerous Environments," in R. Hockey, ed., Stress and Fatigue in Human Performance, Chichester, N.Y.: Wiley, 1983, pp. 123-144.

Ilmarinen J., & Rantanen J. (1999) Promotion of work ability during ageing. American Journal of Industrial Medicine, No. S1, pp. 21-23.

International Labour Organization [ILO] (1986) Psychosocial Factors at Work: Recognition and Control. Occupational Safety and Health Series no: 56, International Labour Office, Geneva.

Isomorphism and collective rationality in organizational field," American Sociological Review, 48, 147-160.

Jackson, S. E., & Schuler, R. S. (1985). A meta-analysis and conceptual critique of research on role ambiguity and role conflict in work settings. Organizational Behaviour and Human Performance, 33, 1-21.

Jamal, M. (1985). Relationship of job stress to job performance: A study of managers and blue Collar workers. Human Relations, 38, 409-424.

Jamal, M., "Relationship of Job Stress to Job Performance: A Study of Managers and Blue-Collar Workers," Human Relations, Vol. 38, 1985, pp. 409-424.

James R. Evans and William M. Lindsay, "The Management and Control of Quality", 4th Edition, South-Western College publishing, p. 177.

Janis, I., and L. Mann, Decision Making, New York: The Free Press, 1977.Jex, S., Stress and Job Performance, Thousand Oaks, Calif.: Sage Publications, 1998.

Janis, I., and L. Mann, Decision Making, New York: The Free Press, 1977.

Jex, S. M. (1998). Stress and job performance: Theory, research, and implications for Managerial practice. Thousand Oaks, CA: Sage.

John Oakland (1995). Total Quality Management, p. 285.

Jones, J.R., Hodgson, J.T., Clegg, T.A. & Elliot R.C. (1998) Self-reported work-related illness in 1995: results from a household survey. Sudbury: HSE Books.

Jones, J. W., Barge, B. N., Steffy, B. D., Fay, L. M., Kunz, L. K., & Wuebker, L. J. (1988). Stress and medical malpractice: Organizational risk assessment and intervention. Journal of Applied Psychology, 73, 727-735.

Juran, J. (1989), Juran on Leadership for Quality, New York, Free Press.

K. Sridhara Bhat (2005): Total Quality Management, Text & Cases, Himalaya.

Keinan, G., "Decision-Making Under Stress: Scanning of Alternatives Under Controllable and Uncontrollable Threats," Journal of Personality and Social Psychology, Vol. 52, No. 3, 1987, pp. 639-644.

Kelly, K. (1992), Quality: Small and midsize companies seize the challenge–not a moment too soon, Business Week, 30, 66-99.

KINES 260–Psychology of Human Movement, Chapter 4, Arousal, Stress and Anxiety

Kjellberg, A., Sköldström, B., Andersson, O., & Lindberg, L. (1996). Fatigue effects of noise on aeroplane mechanics. Work and Stress, 10, 62-71.

Klein, G. (1996). The effect of acute stressors on decision making. In J. E. Driskell & E. Salas (Eds.), Stress and human performance (pp. 49-88). Mahwah, NJ: Lawrence Erlbaum Associates.

Klein, G., "The Effects of Acute Stressors on Decision-Making," in J. Driskell and E. Salas, eds., Stress and Human Performance, Hillsdale, N.J.: Lawrence Erlbaum Associates, 1996, pp. 49-88.

Knoop., R. Reliving stress through value-rich work. Journal of Social Psychology. (1994a) 134, 829-836.

Knoop., R. Work values and job satisfaction. Journal of Psychology (1994b) 128. 683-690.

Kotter, J.P. (1996) Leading Change Boston: Harvard Business School Press.

Landy, F. J. (1992) Work design and stress. In: G. P. Keita & S. L. Sauter (eds.) Work and Well-Being: An Agenda for the 1990s. American Psychological Association, Washington DC.

Larsen, R., "Decision-Making by Military Students Under Extreme Stress," Military Psychology, Vol. 13, No. 2, 2001, pp. 89-92.

Lawler, E.D., S.A Mohrman and E. Ledford Jr. (1998) Strategies for High Performance.

Lazarus, R. S. (1966) Psychological Stress and the Coping Process. McGraw-Hill, New York.

Lazarus, R.S. & Folkman, S. (1984). Stress, Appraisal and Coping. Springer Publications, New York .

Lazarus, R.S., & Folkman, S.(1984). Stress, appraisal and coping. NewYork: Springer Publishing Co.

Lincoln, James R. (1989) Employee Work Attitudes and Management Practice in the US and Japan: Evidence from a Large Comparative Survey. California Management Review, 89-106.

Mallinger, M. as reported in Argyris, C. and Schon, D. A, (1993) Organizational learning II: theory, method and practice, Reading, MA, Addison Wesley.

Mandler, G. (1982) Stress and thought processes. In: L. Goldberg and S. Breznitz (eds.) Handbook of Stress: Theoretical and Clinical Aspects. Free Press, New York.

Mandler, G., "Thought, Memory, and Learning: Effects of Emotional Stress," in L. Goldberger and S. Breznitz, eds., The Handbook of Stress, 2nd edition, New York: The Free Press, 1993.

Matthews, K. A. 1982. "Psychological perspectives on the Type A behaviour pattern." Psychological Bulletin 91: 293-323.

McCraty, R, Atkinsson, M., & Tomasino, D.(2001).Science of the Heart.CA: Institute of Heartmath. Journal 5: 50-55.Jick, T. D., and Payne, R. 1980. "Stress at work." Exchange: The Organizational Behavioural Teaching Journal 5: 50-55.

McGrath, J. E. 1976. "Stress and behaviour in organizations." In Handbook of Industrial and Organizational Psychology. Dunnett, M. D. (ed.) Chicago: Rand McNally College Publishing.: McGraw Hill.

McGrath, J. E., "Stress and Behaviour in Organizations," in M. D. Dunnette, ed., Handbook of Industrial and Organizational Psychology: Vol. 3, 2nd edition, Chicago: Rand McNally, 1976, pp. 1351-1395.

McLeod, P., "A Dual Task Modality Effect: Support for Multiprocessor Models of Attention," Quarterly Journal of Experimental Psychology, Vol. 29, No. 4, November 1977, pp. 651-667.

Meglino, B. M., "Stress and Performance: Are They Always Incompatible?" Supervisory Management, Vol. 22, No. 3, 1977, pp. 2-12.

Meichenbaum, D. (1977) Cognitive-Behaviour Modification. Plenum Press, New York.

Michel Crozier considers the case method as a clinical approach which is a study of particular cases to draw generalizations form the intimate understanding of theses. See Michel Crozier, The Bureaucratic Phenomenon, Chicago, the University of Chicago Press, 1964, pp. 4-5.

Milgram, N., R. Orenstein, and E. Zafrir, "Stressors, Personal Resources, and Social Supports in Military Performance During Wartime," Military Psychology, Vol. 1, No. 4, 1989, pp. 185-199.

Miller, S. (1979). Controllability and human stress: method, evidence and theory. Behavioural Research and Therapy, 17, 28-304.

Miller, D and Hartwick, J. (2002) Administrative fads and their paradoxical properties, Unpublished paper.

Morrison, E. W. and Milliken, F. J. (2000) Organizational silence: A barrier to change and development in a pluralistic world, Academy of Management Review, 25, 4, 706-725.

Motowidlo, S. J., Packard, J. S., & Manning, M. R. (1986). Occupational stress: Its causes and consequences on job performance. Journal of Applied Psychology, 71, 618-629.

Murphy, L.R. (1988) Workplace interventions for stress reduction and prevention. In CL Cooper & R. Payne (eds.) Causes, Coping and Consequences of Stress at Work.

Murphy, L.R., Hurrell, J.J. & Quick, J.C. (1992) Work and well-being: where do we go from here? In J.C. Quick, L.R. Murphy, & J.J. Hurrell (eds.) Stress and Well-being at Work: Assessments and Interventions for Occupational Mental Health. American Psychological Association, Washington DC.

Muse, L., S. Harris, and H. Field, "Has the Inverted-U Theory of Stress and Job Performance Had a Fair Test?" Human Performance, Vol. 16, No. 4, September 2003, pp. 349-364.

Nonaka, I., Takeuchi, H. (1995) The Knowledge-Creating Company: How Japanese Companies Create the Dynamics of Innovation. New York: Oxford University Press.

NTPC is maintaining quality and professional circles for about two decades which form part of TQM.`Organ, D. W. 1979. "The meaning of stress." Business Horizons 6: 32-40.

Norman Gaither, Greg Frazier, Production and Operations Management, 9th Edition, South-Western College Publishing, p. 649.

Orpen., C. Interactive effects of work motivation and personal control on employee job performance and satisfaction. Journal of Social Psychology (1994), Vol. 134 (6), 855-856.

Palmer S. Managing Stress. Conference paper given at the Chartered Institute of personnel and Development, Harrogate, UK, 25th October 2001. Sutherland V, Cooper CL. Strategic Stress Management: An Organisational Approach. London :Macmillan Books, 2001. pp. 238-244.

Parasuraman, S., and Alutto, J. A. 1984. "Sources and outcomes of stress in organizational settings: Toward the development of a structural model." Academy of Management Journal 27: 330-350.

Pauline V. Young–Scientific Social Surveys and Research, p. 247.

Payne, R. (1991). Individual differences in cognition and the stress process. In C. L. Cooper & R. Payne (eds.), Personality and stress: Individual differences in the stress process (pp. 181-204). New York: Wiley.

Pearlin, L., & Schooler, C. (1978). The structure of coping. Journal of Health and Social Behaviour, 19, 2-21.

Pearlin, L., Lieberman, M. L., Menaghan, E., & Mullan, J. T. (1981) The stress process. Journal of Health and Social Behaviour, 19, 2-21.

Performance Organizations: Employee Involvement, TQM and Reengineering Programs in Fortune 1000 Corporations, San Francisco, Jossey-Bass.

Perkins, D. V. (1988) The assessment of stress using life events scales. In: L. Gold-berg & S Breznitz (eds.) Handbook of Stress: Theoretical and Clinical Aspects. Free Press, New York.

Perls, F. S., 1969. Gestalt Therapy Verbatim. Lafayette, CA: Real People Press.

Petersen, Peter B. (1999) Total Quality Management And The Deming Approach

Postman, L., & Bruner, J. S. (1948). Perception under stress. Psychological Review, 55, 314-323.

Prakash, M.S., Esteva, G. (1998) Escaping Education: Living as Learning within Grassroots Cultures. New York: Peter Lang. Publishing House, pp. 4-5.

Quick, J. C., and Quick, J. D. 1984. Organizational Stress and Preventive Management. New York: McGraw-Hill.

Rahe, R. H. (1969) Multi-cultural correlations of life change scaling: America, Japan, Denmark, and Sweden. Journal of Psychosomatic Research, 13, 191-195.

Raju Arisetti: Stress Strikes Corporate World, Economic Times Esquire, October, 28, 1989, p. 1.

Richard B. Chase, Nicholas J. Aquilaus and F. Robert Jacobs, Production and Operation Management, Inrwin McGraw-Hill, 8th Edition, p. 201.

Richard B. Chase, Nicholas J. Aquilaus and F. Robert Jacobs, Ronda Roberts Callister and James A. Wall, Jr., "Conflict across Organisational boundaries: Managed Care Organisations versus Health Care Providers," Journal of Applied Psychology, Vol. 86, No. 4, 2001, pp. 754-763.

Robert K. Yin. Case Study Research. Design and Methods. Third Edition. Applied social research method series Volume 5. Sage Publications. California, 2002.

Rosch, Paul (1999). Stress, Headache, and other Head Pain. Health and Stress, 3, 1-8.

Rosenstock, L. (1997) Work organization research at the National Institute for Occupational Safety and Health. Journal of Occupational Health Psychology, 2(1), 7-100.

Salo, K. (1995) Teacher stress and coping over an autumn term in Finland. Work & Stress, 9 (1), 55-66.

Sanders, A. F., "Towards a Model for Stress and Human Performance," Acta Psychologica, Vol.53, 1983, pp. 61-97.

Schaffer, R. H. (1998) The breakthrough strategy: Using short term success to build the high performance organization, Cambridge, Ballinger Publishing.

Schaffer, R. H. (1998) The breakthrough strategy: Using short term success to build the high performance organization, Cambridge, Ballinger Publishing.

Schein, E. H. (1992) Organizational culture and leadership, San Francisco, Jossey-Bass.

Scheuch, K. (1990): Psychosoziale Faktoren im Arbeitsprozeß und Gesundheit: Einführung.Z. ges. Hyg. 36, 403-407.

Scheuch, K. (1996): Stress and resources at work in a changing society. Bremerhaven: Wirtschaftsverlag NW, pp.95-109 (Schriftenreihe der Bundesanstalt für Arbeitsmedizin:Tagungsbericht 11).

Schonpflug, F. & Battmann, A. (1988) The costs and benefits of coping. In: S. Fisher & J. Reason (eds.) Handbook of Life Stress, Cognition and Health. Wiley & Son, Chichester.

Scott, D.F., Martin, J.D., Petty, J.W., and Keown, A.J. (1999) Basic Financial Management. New Jersey: Prentice Hall International Inc.

Scott, W. E., Jr., "Activation Theory and Task Design," Organizational Behaviour and Human Performance, No. 1, 1966, pp. 3-30.

Searle, B. J., Bright, J. E. H., & Bochner, S. (1999). Testing the 3-factor model of occupational stress: the impact of demands, control and social support on a mail sorting task. Work and Stress, 13, 268-279.

Selye, H. (1950) Physiology and Pathology of expose to stress. Montreal: Acta.

Selye, H. The Stress of Life, New York: McGraw-Hill, 1956.

Selye, H. (1936) A syndrome produced by diverse nocuous agents. Nature, 138.

Selye, H. (1950) Stress, Acta Incorporated, Montreal.

Selye, H., Stress Without Distress, New York: JP Lippicott Company, 1975.

Selye, H., "History of the Stress Concept," in L. Goldberger and S. Breznitz, eds., The Handbook of Stress, 2nd edition, New York: The Free Press, 1993.

Senge, Peter (1993) The Fifth Discipline: The Art and Practice of the Learning Organization.

Sevelius, G. 1986. "Experience with preventative measures." In Occupational Stress. Wolf, S. G., Jr. and Finerstone, A. J. (eds.) p. 191-211. Littleton, MA: PSG Publishing.

Shaham, Y., J. Singer, and M. Schaeffer, "Stability/Instability of Cognitive Strategies Across Tasks Determine Whether Stress Will Affect Judgmental Processes," Journal of Applied Psychology, Vol. 22, No. 9, 1992, pp. 691-713.

Shaw, J. B., & Weekley, J. A. (1985). The effects of objective work-load variations of psychological strain and post-work-load performance. Journal of Management, 11, 87-98.

Shepard, Jon; Robert W. Greene (2003). Sociology and You. Ohio: Glencoe McGraw-Hill. p. A-22.

Siegfried Lamnek. Qualitative Sozialforschung. Lehrbuch. 4. Auflage. Beltz Verlag. Weihnhein, Basel, 2005.

Spector, B. and Beer, M. (1994) Beyond TQM programmes, Journal of Organizational Change, 7, 2, 63-70.

Spector, P. E., Dwyer, D. J., & Jex, S. M. (1988). Relation of job stressors to affective, health, and performance outcomes: A comparison of multiple data sources. Journal of Applied Psychology, 73, 11-19.

Sperandio, J. C. (1971). Variation of operator's strategies and regulating effects on workload. Ergonomics, 14, 571-577.

Spielberger, C.D. (1976) The nature and measurement of anxiety. In C.D. Spielberger and R. Diaz-Guerrero (eds.) Cross-Cultural Anxiety. Hemisphere, Washington DC.

Srivastava, A. K., and A. Krishna, "A Test of Inverted U Hypothesis of Stress Performance Relationship in the Industrial Context," Psychological Studies, Vol. 34, 1991, pp. 34-38.

Srivastava, A.K. (1991). A study of role stress-mental health relationship as moderated by adopted coping strategies. Psychological Studies, 36 (3), 192-197.

Staw, B.M. and L.D. Epstein (2000) What bandwagons bring: Effects of popular management techniques on corporate performance, reputation and CEO pay, Administrative Science Quarterly, 45, 523-556.

Staw, R. M., L. E. Sandelands, and J. E. Dutton, "Threat-Rigidity Effects in Organizational Behaviour: A Multi-Level Analysis," Administrative Quarterly, No. 26, 1981, pp. 501-524.

Surtees P.G. & Wainwright N.W.J (1998) Adversity over the life course: assessment and quantification issues. Stress Medicine, vol. 14, no. 4, pp. 205-211.

Sutherland, V. J., & Cooper, CL (1990) Understanding stress: psychological perspective for health professionals. Psychology &Health, series: 5. Chapman and Hall, London.

Tiblao., T.A. Work motivation and productivity of Government workers. Philippine Journal of Psychology (1990), Vol. 23, 30-38.

To Quality Management. Journal of Management History 5, 8, 468-488.

Tubbs, T. C., & Collins, J. M. (2000). Jackson and Schuler (1985) revisited: a meta-analysis of the relationships between role ambiguity, role conflict, and job performance. Journal of Management, 26, 155-169.

Van der Hek, H. & Plomp, H.N. (1997) Occupational stress

management programmes: a practical overview of published effect studies. Occupational Medicine, 47 (3), 133-141.

Virginia M. Gibson: Stress in Work Place: A Hidden Cost Factor, H.R.Focus, January, 1993, p. 15.

Vroom, V. H., Work and Motivation, New York: Wiley Press, 1964.

Westman, M., & Eden, D. (1996). The inverted-U relationship between stress and performance: a Field study. Work and Stress, 10, 165-173.

Westphal, J.D., Gulati, R. and Shortell, S. M. (1997) Customization or conformity? An institutional and network perspective on the content and consequences of TQM adoptions, Administrative Science Quarterly, 42, 366-394.

Williams, J. C., and Huber, G. P. 1986. Human Behaviour in Organizations. Cincinnati, OH: South-Western Publishing.

World Health Organization (2003). Authored by: Cassitto, M.G., Fattorini, E., Gilioni, R., Rengo, C. & Gonik, V. 'Raising Awareness of Psychological Harassment at Work'. Geneva: WHO, 2003(Protecting Workers' Health series No. 4). Geneva: WHO.

World Health Organization (2004). Authored by: Leka, S., Griffiths, A. & Cox, T. Work Organization and Stress: Systematic problem approaches for employers, managers and trade unions representatives. Geneva: WHO (Protecting Workers' Health series 3). Geneva: World Health Organization (WHO).

World Health Organization [WHO] (1986) Constitution of the World Health Organization. In: Basic Documents (36th ed). World Health Organization, Geneva.

Wykes, J. & Whittington, R. (1991) Coping strategies used by staff following assault by a patient: an exploratory study. Work & Stress, 5 (1), 37-48.

Yerkes, R., and J. Dodson, "The Relation of Strength of Stimulus to Rapidity of Habit Formation," Journal of Comparative Neurology and Psychology, Vol. 18, 1908, pp. 459-482.

Zack, M. (1999) Developing a Knowledge Strategy. California Management Review. 41, 125-144.

Zbaracki, M. J. (1998) The rhetoric and reality of total quality management," Administrative Science Quarterly, 43, 602-638.

Zivnuska, S., C. Kiewitz, and W. Hochwarter, "What Is Too Much or Too Little? The Curvilinear Effects of Job Tension on Turnover Intent, Value Attainment, and Job Satisfaction," Journal of Applied Psychology, Vol. 32, No. 7, July 2002, pp. 1334-1360.

Index

Index